When a
Man
Loves a
Woman

When a Man Loves a Woman

God's Design for Relationships

James Ford Jr.

MOODY PUBLISHERS
CHICAGO

Library of Congress Cataloging-in-Publication Data

Ford, James, 1951-
    When a man loves a woman: pursuing her heart / by James Ford, Jr.
        p. cm.
    Includes bibliographical references
    ISBN 0-8024-6839-X
        1. Men—Religious Life. 2. Love—Religious Aspects—Christianity.
    3. Man-women relationships—Religious aspects—Christianity. I. Title.

BV4440.F67 2004
248.8'425—dc22

2004009699

3 5 7 9 10 8 6 4 2

Printed in the United States of America

This book is dedicated to my wife Leslie Ann Ford. She is my "12th" Rose and the inspiration behind the writing of it. She is my faithful friend, loyal confidant, dutiful wife, loving mother, extraordinary grandmother and the sole object of my affection. I thank God for her.

So Jacob went on his journey and came to the land of the people of the East. And he looked, and saw a well in the field; and behold, there were three flocks of sheep lying by it; for out of that well they watered the flocks. A large stone was on the well's mouth. Now all the flocks would be gathered there; and they would roll the stone from the well's mouth, water the sheep, and put the stone back in its place on the well's mouth.

And Jacob said to them, "My brethren, where are you from?" And they said, "We are from Haran." Then he said to them, "Do you know Laban the son of Nahor?" And they said, "We know him." So he said to them, "Is he well?" And they said, "He is well. And look, his daughter Rachel is coming with the sheep."

Then he said, "Look, it is still high day; it is not time for the cattle to be gathered together. Water the sheep, and go and feed them." But they said, "We cannot until all the flocks are gathered together, and they have rolled the stone from the well's mouth; then we water the sheep."

Now while he was still speaking with them, Rachel came with her father's sheep, for she was a shepherdess. And it came to pass, when Jacob saw Rachel the daughter of Laban his mother's brother, and the sheep of Laban his mother's brother, that Jacob went near and rolled the stone from the well's mouth, and watered the flock of Laban his mother's brother. Then Jacob kissed Rachel, and lifted up his voice and wept. And Jacob told Rachel that he was her father's relative and that he was Rebekah's son. So she ran and told her father.

Then it came to pass, when Laban heard the report about Jacob his sister's son, that he ran to meet him, and embraced him and kissed him, and brought him to his house. So he told Laban all these things. And Laban said to him, "Surely you are my bone and my flesh." And he stayed with him for a month.

Genesis 29:1–14 NKJV

CONTENTS

INTRODUCTION

$\mathcal{S}$ome of you may remember the phenomenon we used to call a "house party." All evening long you got your groove on, dancing with anyone willing to dance with you—that is, until the end of the party. That last dance was always a slow one, played against a backdrop of dimmed lights and emotion, reserved for couples who danced too close for comfort.

I remember one occasion when I could hardly wait for the last dance. The lyrics of the current hit song "When a Man Loves a Woman" by Percy Sledge, would tell "Pug" (pronounced Pudge), also known as Leslie, the woman who would eventually become my wife, everything I had in my heart for her.

The song tells the story of a brother in love. He is totally preoccupied. His nose is open. He can't think of anything or anyone else but her. There isn't anything he wouldn't do or sacrifice to be with her. She is wonderful! The sun, moon, stars, and planets all revolve around her. She's perfect. If he could change anything about her, he wouldn't, because she can do no wrong. If she did something wrong, he'd never notice. If anyone ever tried to bring her shortcomings to his attention, they'd run the risk of losing his friendship, since the woman he loved was perfect.

Nothing was too good for her. He'd spend all of his money on her. If she said, "Jump," he'd ask, "How high?" He begged her to treat him right, since he was totally and completely at her mercy.

"Don't play me!" he'd plead, because he knew she had the power and opportunity. If she ever decided to treat him bad, he'd be the very last to know, because he was so caught up in his feelings for her . . .

Someone once said, "Love is a feeling, and when you feel it, you feel like you've never felt before." Sometimes love just feels amorphous. It is beyond measure. Love can be demonstrated in many ways. Yet, its description and definition are elusive.

Throughout history men have gone to great lengths to demonstrate love. Real love will cause a man to behave in ways that he would not normally consider rational, just as the lyrics to "When a Man Loves a Woman" imply.

If you are a baby boomer (born between 1940 and 1960) or older, you may remember Charles Boyer. He was the suave, dapper, handsome, and graceful leading man to some of the most famous and beautiful starlets of the silver screen. However, that persona was reserved for the camera and fan magazines. In real life, Charles loved only one woman: his wife, Patricia. Everyone that knew Charles and Pat maintained that they had a lifelong love affair. They were no less lovers, friends, and companions after forty-four years of marriage than they were in their first year together.

When Patricia developed liver cancer, Charles could not bear for her to know her true condition, so for six months he sat by her bedside day and night, providing hope and cheer. Patricia eventually died in his arms. Two days after her death, Charles died by his own hand. He left a note that read, "Her love was life to me. All I've ever wanted in life was Pat. Now she's gone and life has no more meaning."

Charles Boyer was a man upon whose words and movements millions of women were fixed. Yet, he was not interested in any other woman, because he was in love with his wife. Nothing could distract or dissuade him. Charles thought of no one else. Though the winds of time, sickness, and death blew hard enough to snatch his beloved from his arms, nothing could take her from his heart.

Charles Boyer's story is tragic. Equally as tragic as not being able to let go of a loved one in death is the all-too-typical tragedy that occurs when a man thinks he loves a woman, or a woman thinks a man loves her, and he doesn't. Let me illustrate this dilemma using a few of the "Top 20 R & B" singles, as listed in a recent issue of *Jet* magazine:

Like Mariah Carey, you said, "Thank God I Found You," because he insisted, like Genuine, "I'm the Best Man That I Could Be." As the artist formerly known as Prince declared, you said, "I Have Found the Man for Me" and "The Greatest Romance Ever," and that despite his faults.

In response to his flaws you intoned, like Faith Evans, "Love Is Blind." You thought there was only ease and clear skies on your horizon, similar to Angie Stone. "No More Rain" was your anthem.

Your mantra was in unison with Black: "Bring It All to Me." What else was there to do but say yes, when he declared, "Let's Get Married" (Jagged Edge), and, like Montell Jordan, "Get It On Tonite!"

The only thing left for you to ask was "Say My Name" (Destiny's Child).

Sadly, as his faults came more to the surface, you heard Jagged Edge warn: "He Can't Love You."

You realized that J-Shin was right—his love is just a "One Night Stand," because "He Wasn't Man Enough" (Toni Braxton).

Many young people believe Michael Bolton was the first artist to sing "When a Man Loves a Woman," but actually it was written, produced, and recorded by two others before Michael was born. Percy Sledge arranged the familiar tune in 1966, but Jacob of the Old Testament penned the first version in the 29th chapter of Genesis.

Everyone knows that Jacob of the Old Testament was a rascal, a supplanter, and a deceiver, but Jacob knew how to do one thing very well . . . Jacob knew how to love a woman.

Jacob *won* Rachel's heart. He was willing to *work* and *wait* to *wed* the only woman he ever *wanted*. Finally, because of his sincere commitment to protect their love, Jacob *warned* Rachel.

It is my sincere hope that Jacob's life will serve as a yardstick to assist Christian men in general, single Christian men in particular, in evaluating the length, breadth, width, and height of your love for the women you hold dear. May the Lord give you comprehension of His Word as you prayerfully consider what the Scriptures have to say about what happens *When a Man Loves a Woman.*

Chapter One

THE JACOB AND RACHEL STORY

The well was a regular place of work. It was neither extraordinary nor supernatural. Scripture reveals that it was customary for Rachel to go to the well to water her father's sheep.

DISCOVER AND FULFILL GOD'S PURPOSE FOR YOUR LIFE

It was in the course of her normal, daily activity that Jacob discovered Rachel. Rachel did not waste time peering into a pool of water at her reflection, day-dreaming about a speculative suitor. Like Rachel, singles must diligently pursue and perfect the gifts, talents, ministry, and vocation that God has uniquely ordained for them. Second Peter 1:5–7 outlines the training sequence prescribed by God:

Giving all diligence, add to your faith virtue; and to virtue knowledge; and to knowledge temperance; and to temperance patience; and to patience godliness; and to godliness brotherly kindness; and to brotherly kindness charity.

Add to Your Faith

There are basic skills that every growing Christian should master—most notably, the ability to lead a person to Christ and encourage them to maturity. Others include teaching (2 Timothy 1:11), preaching (1 Timothy 2:7), counseling (2 Corinthians 1:4), and serving (Romans 1:1). However, genuine ministry and unearthing God's call on our lives grows out of a walk of faith! Faith is perceiving what God wants us to accomplish and living our lives in accordance with those objectives. It is the foundation on which virtue, knowledge, temperance, patience, godliness, brotherly kindness, and genuine love are established.

Rachel was busy doing the work set before her, wisely "redeeming the time" (Ephesians 5:15–16).

Genesis 29:10 says that when Jacob saw Rachel, he literally saw with comprehension. It was love at first sight! The Hebrew word translated "saw" in Genesis 29:10 literally means "to see with comprehension." Of course, there are those who do not believe in love at first sight. They say you must take a second and sometimes a third look. Perhaps there is some truth in the saying, "Puppy love can lead to a dog's life." I can relate to Jacob, however, because my personal experience mirrors his.

When I first saw Leslie forty years ago (when she was eight years old), I knew she would grow up and become my wife. I told her so the very first day I met her. Of course, I don't recommend that everyone propose to his intended the first time they meet, but I do believe that it is possible to recognize your life partner instantly.

THE RELEVANCE OF RACHEL'S OUTWARD APPEARANCE

When Genesis chapter 29 introduces Rachel, it doesn't speak of her character: "Rachel was lovely in form, and beautiful. Jacob was in love with Rachel" (29:17–18 NIV). By declaring Jacob's love right after mentioning her appearance, the implication is Rachel's beauty was, at the least, a minimal consideration in his declaration of love. Although beauty often attracts love, it doesn't end there.

The Eye of the Beholder

When a man looks at a woman, his perception is overwhelmingly influenced by the emotion he feels for the one his gaze is fixed on. A man in love *sees the woman he loves as beautiful.* Studies suggest that being objectively attractive is less important to a woman's well-being than *feeling* attractive and being *treated* as attractive by a loving beholder. [1]

I think we can conclude that women don't have to *be* beautiful, but they need to be loved in ways that make them *feel* beautiful! The curious gazer can uncover beauty. He doesn't dream of conquest, but of discovery. He is like an explorer. He isn't interested in possessing his woman or exploiting her resources. Instead he wants to learn of her and delight in her.

It was with a curious gaze of delight that Adam first beheld Eve. She was unique, unlike any of the other creatures in his world. She moved him to wonder. Women long to be looked at the way Adam looked at Eve and Jacob gazed at Rachel: with enraptured pleasure.

If beauty is in the eye of the beholder, then a loving beholder must have the power to bring out the beauty in his beloved. In the movie *The Cooler* starring Alec Baldwin, the cooler told his girlfriend—who had been disfigured on her face—not to judge her beauty by looking in the mirror, but by looking into his eyes. Then she would truly know how beautiful she is. A husband's words of affirmation and praise have the power to turn his wife into a Rachel![2]

JACOB LOVED RACHEL UNCONDITIONALLY

The first time he laid eyes on her, Jacob knew Rachel was the woman he wanted to be his wife. His motivation for wanting to marry Rachel was *his love for her.* Genesis 29:18 says, "Jacob loved Rachel," Genesis 29:20 says Jacob loved Rachel, and Genesis 29:30 says Jacob loved Rachel. The word used to describe Jacob's love for Rachel is *hesed* in the Old Testament and is equivalent to the New Testament word *agape.*

Five words are translated "love" in the New Testament. God makes these distinctions to precisely communicate feeling, purpose, and meaning.

Phileo (friendship)—To cherish and have a tender affection for the beloved. It anticipates a response. Comradeship. Sharing. Communication. Friendship. *Phileo* is shared by dear friends who enjoy closeness and companionship. A marriage without *phileo* will be lacking, even if there is passion, since *phileo* flavors the marriage with common interests, goals, and objectives.

Storge (family love)—A natural affection and a sense of belonging to each other that is shared and expressed among parents, children, brothers, and sisters. *Storge* provides an atmosphere of security in which other forms of married love can flourish.

Epitumia (physical love)—Although not translated "love," *epitumia* is a critical aspect of married love. It denotes a strong physical desire. While not the most important aspect, it can be an indicator of the health of a marriage.

Eros (romantic love)—It includes the idea of yearning to unite with and please the loved one. Romantic, passionate, and sentimental. The kind of love poets write about in songs and poems. Exquisite pleasure. Strong. Sweet and sometimes terrifying. *Eros* is wholly emotional and cannot be summoned at will. It cannot be independent and will die if not combined with the other types of love to rejuvenate and strengthen it. *Eros* transforms a mere existence into a glorious adventure.

Finally, there is *agape*. The totally unselfish love that has the capacity to give and keep giving without expectation of anything being given in return. *Agape* values and serves in contrast to phileo, which cherishes and enjoys. *Agape* is the love that you can bring to marriage immediately, since it is extended as a choice of your will independent of emotion. *Agape* love is supernatural and goes on operating when every other kind of love is lacking.

The love Jacob had for Rachel was genuine *agape*. It wasn't an "if you love me" or "because you love me" kind of love, but it was an unconditional and "in spite of" kind of a love, the highest kind of love anyone can demonstrate. When a man *really* loves a woman, he does not love her for how she looks, what she can do for him, how she makes him feel, or even because she loves him with the same measure he loves her. This superior love is given without regard to individual achievement and superior qualities. This Jacob-style of love is not a reward for these. Looks, ability to help, and feelings are not the reason *agape* is given. Jacob loved Rachel for the sake of loving her. He delighted in his love for her exclusively. When a man loves a woman, he just loves her.

Jacob's expression of love toward Rachel was not unique in his day, and it is not unique today. I agree with Edith Deen who wrote in *All the Women of the Bible:* "Jacob's words are unsurpassed in the whole of romantic love literature. In fact, Jacob's service for Rachel marks him as the most devoted lover in the Bible. His love for Rachel was not a passing fancy; it would last until the end of his life." [3]

Now, let's look at what happens as Jacob *wins, works* for, *waits* on, *wants, weds,* and *warns* Rachel. These are the objectives a man has the tenacity to accomplish when he truly loves a woman.

Chapter Two

WHEN A MAN LOVES A WOMAN
He Wins Her by
Affirming Her Identity

> *And it came to pass, when Jacob saw Rachel*
> *the daughter of Laban his mother's brother, and*
> *the sheep of Laban his mother's brother, that*
> *Jacob went near and rolled the stone from the*
> *well's mouth, and watered the flock of Laban*
> *his mother's brother.*
>
> *Genesis 29:10*

An old Jewish proverb paints a good picture of God's ordained plan that a woman's identity is distinct from a man's: "The woman was not taken from the man's head to be over him, nor from his feet to be walked on by him, but from his side to be his closest companion, from under his arm to be protected by him, near his heart to be loved by him."

God confirms this wise saying in Genesis 2:23 (NIV): "I will make a helper suitable for him." When Adam saw his gift, Eve, he said, "This is now bone of my bones and flesh of my flesh; she shall be called Woman." Why didn't Adam call her his wife? He would have been correct; she was his wife. Why woman? Because God is establishing a principle for all women, not just wives.

Adam is affirming her identity, distinct from his. Eve is a woman whether she is a wife or not. Like all women,

Eve needs her femininity affirmed. God tells us in Genesis 3 that women have unique tastes and preferences: "The woman saw that the tree was good for food, and that it was pleasant to the eyes." Woman is made soft. Man is made hard. The Hebrew name for woman is *ishshah,* which means soft and sculptured. The Hebrew word for man is *ish,* which means hard.

So then, how can a man affirm a woman's unique identity?

THE FEMININE HEART

In *Wild at Heart: Discovering the Secret of a Man's Soul,* John Eldredge states it this way:

> There are . . . three desires that I have found essential to a woman's heart, which are not entirely different from a man's and yet they remain distinctly feminine. Not every woman wants a battle to fight, but every woman yearns to be fought for. Listen to the longing of a woman's heart: She wants to be pursued. "I just want to be a priority to someone," a friend in her thirties told me.
>
> And her childhood dreams of a knight in shining armor coming to rescue her are not girlish fantasies; they are the core of the feminine heart and the life she knows she was made for.
>
> Every woman also wants an adventure to share. Many men make the mistake of thinking that the woman is the adventure; she wants to be caught up in something greater than herself.
>
> Finally, every woman wants to have her beauty unveiled. Not to conjure, but to unveil. There is also a deep desire to simply and truly be the beauty, and be delighted in. Most little girls will remember playing

dress up, or wedding day, or twirling in skirts—those flowing dresses that were perfect for spinning around in. She'll put her pretty dress on, come into the living room and twirl. What she longs for is to capture her daddy's delight. My wife remembers standing on top of the coffee table as a girl of five or six, and singing her heart out. *Do you see me?* asks the heart of every girl. *And are you captivated by what you see?*

The world kills a woman's heart when it tells her to be tough, efficient and independent. . . . All we've offered the feminine soul is pressure to be a "good servant." No one is fighting for her heart; there is no grand adventure to be swept up in; and every woman doubts very much that she has any beauty to unveil.

Delight in Her Beauty

First, a man can make a woman feel special by delighting in her beauty. As I stated earlier, beauty is the outward expression of the inward reality! There are some women who are obviously stunning, but even they exude an additional "shine" when looked upon and made beautiful by "the face of love"—her man's loving face that sees the woman as beautiful because he loves her. Remember, if beauty is in the eye of the beholder, then the loved woman radiates the beauty of security, and so her face can be called the "face of love."[4] We give back to the world a reflection of the love we have received. The face of love, then, is the face of one who is loved.

Give Gifts That Communicate High Value

To value something is to attach great importance to it. God gave me a great idea to help me affirm my wife's

identity and communicate to her what a priceless trea-
sure she is to me. I have been doing it at least once a year
for the past nine years. I'll never forget the first time I
blessed Leslie with one of her special days. I called one
of her best friends, Maria, and told her to invite my wife
out shopping. It was an invitation I knew my wife could
not refuse. I even offered to pay for the entire shopping
spree, gave her $50, and sent her on her way! While she
was out, I cleaned the house from top to bottom and
sprayed Leslie's favorite cologne through-out the house.
I asked Maria to give me a call prior to bringing my wife
home. I warned her not to accompany my wife to the
door, because if she did, she would see her pastor as
she'd never seen him before!

Leslie's eyes were wide with surprise when she stepped
through the door and was greeted with, "Madam, your
servant awaits your every command," as I bowed. In
Hebrew, to "bow the knee" is the root meaning of *blessing*. Bowing before someone is a graphic picture of valu-
ing that person. Leslie squealed with glee when she saw
a dozen roses in the living room, a dozen in the dining
room, and a dozen in the kitchen. Of course, the bow tie
around my neck, towel over my arm, and silk boxers
didn't hurt!

I relieved her of her bags . . . and clothing. I placed
a robe around her as I led her to the bathroom, where
there were another dozen roses. The aroma of peach
bubble bath (her favorite) drifted through the bathroom.

I helped her into the tub and began to bathe her. As
I gingerly washed her, I began to tell her how much I appreciated her and the sacrifices she had made through-
out our married life. I reminded her how she gave up her
home in Pittsburgh to accompany me to Chicago to train
for ministry. I thanked her for giving up her educational goals in order for me to attain my degrees. I remind-

ed her how she gave up her job and good career to stay at home just so that our teenage boys would have a parent at home after school. I looked lovingly into her tear-filled eyes and began to weep as well. Our silence was deafening. It was a moment neither of us will ever forget. It is indelibly etched in our minds. I dried her off, and we put on robes and headed for our bedroom, where we dined on stuffed Cornish hens, cheese broccoli rolls made from scratch, and baked Alaska for dessert. What happened next is none of your business!

BESTOWING A BLESSING

The two primary elements of the special day I gave Leslie were spoken words and meaningful touch. [5]

Spoken Words

For many Christians, words of love and acceptance are seldom heard. It is a tragedy that we withhold kindness from each other in the body of Christ, in our friendships, and in our homes. For some there is a common misconception that "just being there" communicates acceptance and blessing. Not true! More often than not, silence communicates a cavalier attitude and confusion. This is especially true for children. When they are left to fill in the blanks for themselves, they frequently arrive at the wrong conclusion. Sadly, they do not lack for negative verbal messages that their peers are quick to impart.

Abraham blessed Isaac. Isaac blessed Jacob. Jacob gave a verbal blessing to each of his twelve sons and to two of his grandchildren. God has blessed us with the gift of His Word. He has always been a God of the spoken word. When Jesus was baptized, God spoke audibly,

25

confirming His great pleasure with the Son: "And lo a voice from heaven, saying, This is my beloved Son, in whom I am well pleased" (Matthew 3:17). We must speak blessings. Good words are necessary to assure our loved ones of our genuine, unconditional acceptance.

Meaningful Touch

Touch is a vital element in bestowing a blessing. In Old Testament homes, it was always given in concert with spoken words. Kissing, hugging, and laying on of hands were all included in giving affirmation and blessing. The act of touch is significant in communicating warmth, personal acceptance—even physical health.

Over one-third of our five million touch receptors are centered in our hands![6] Interestingly, laying on of hands has become a curiosity to the medical community. Dr. Dolores Krieger, professor of nursing at New York University, has done copious research on the effects of laying on of hands. Dr. Krieger discovered that the toucher and the one being touched receive physiological benefits. This is possible because the hemoglobin that carries oxygen to the tissues is invigorated, receiving more oxygen. This increase in oxygen energizes a person and can even aid in the regenerative process if they are sick.[7]

Further studies confirm that meaningful touch can increase immunity, lower blood pressure, and even add up to two years to your life. A study conducted at UCLA found that just to maintain emotional and physical health, men and women need eight to ten meaningful touches each day![8] Meaningful touch is a profound way to impart blessing.

Chapter Three

WHEN A MAN LOVES A WOMAN

He Wins Her by Showing Appreciation for Her Vocation

*J*acob really cared for Rachel! Genesis 29:10 states, "And it came to pass, when Jacob saw Rachel the daughter of Laban his mother's brother, that Jacob *went near,* and rolled the stone from the well's mouth and watered the flock of Laban his mother's brother" (italics mine).

The words "went near" are actually one word in Hebrew. Moses used the word in Exodus 19:15 in the present perfect tense: "And he said unto the people, be ready against the third day: *come* not at your wives" (italics mine). The word is *nagash,* and it carries an emotional connotation. Moses uses it to instruct the Israelites to avoid romantic intimacy with their wives as part of their preparation to receive the Law of God.

REMOVING HINDRANCES TO HER SUCCESS

In regard to Rachel, *nagash* denotes the intensity of Jacob's loving concern that Rachel be able to accomplish the task before her. Jacob demonstrated that he cared about Rachel's ability to accomplish the work delegated to her by moving the stone from the mouth of the well so she could water her father's flock. His actions said, "As a woman, you should not have to move the stone, nor should you be hindered by it, Rachel. Please allow me to help you so that you can complete your work and fulfill the purpose your father has given you to accomplish today."

Help the Woman in Your Life Discover Her Purpose

The greatest way to destroy someone is to distract her from her true purpose. Conversely, the best way to encourage a person's success is to help her discover her life purpose. It is the desire of God's heart that each person He has given life to would accomplish the purpose that He created them for. "The plans of the LORD stand firm forever, the purposes of his heart through all generations" (Psalm 33:11 NIV).

God has purposes that He has ordained will be carried out by humanity in general, as well as purposes for men, purposes for women, and purposes for children. God has specific tasks for men to perform and women to accomplish, work that is uniquely designed for each individual. We are not the result of some divine experiment. In fact, discovering God's purpose for our lives is the key to personal satisfaction and fulfillment.[9] When a man loves a woman, he will be committed to helping her discover the life purpose that God has placed in her heart and mind.

The Woman's Purpose Revealed

Receive Love. The primary purpose of the woman was to receive love from the man, just as God's major purpose for creating man was to receive love from God. God and man maintained their spiritual relationship, but God wanted man to have someone that he could share soul-love with. Adam had a void of intimacy. He needed to share life with humanity socially, spiritually, emotionally, and physically. "It is not good for the man to be alone. I will make a helper suitable for him" (Genesis 2:18 NIV). A woman's body reflects her role as receiver. Her ability to receive complements the man's role to give.

'Fit.' Meet as used in Genesis 2:18 (KJV) actually means "fit." The implication is that the woman was a perfect match for the man. As stated earlier, men and women need each other to fulfill our mutual purposes and for balance, whether married or single! [10]

The vitality that comes from the contribution of women should not be ignored. Women frequently have an alertness or caution in their spirit. This is frequently referred to as "intuition." There are many examples of this in Scripture.

The wife of a prosperous landowner in Shunem precisely discerned Elisha's godly character and urged her husband to assist him (2 Kings 4:8–10). The wife of a governing ruler in Jerusalem discerned the innocent character of Jesus and warned her husband not to proceed with rendering a judgment against Him (Matthew 27:19).

Have Faith. Faith is not "a shot in the dark." Rather, it is discerning what God's intended purpose is and accomplishing that purpose. More often than not, God reveals His purpose gradually in direct correspondence to how well we obey.

I liken the exercising of faith to following a narrowly lit path. I would love to have one of those huge search lights that the police use to illuminate an entire neighborhood from a helicopter. Experience has taught me, however, that God usually gives me about the amount of light that I can expect to have from a flashlight, just enough for the step in front of me. I get light for the next step as I take the one preceding in obedience! Faith is a dynamic enablement that gives an individual the desire and power to accomplish God's will.

Create. Creativity is the ability to see a need, task, or idea from a unique perspective, and then meet it. Incumbent in this is honing in on the natural gifts and abilities God has bestowed on each individual. When a man loves a woman, he observes and appreciates her gifts and encourages her in them. Where is she going? What is she supposed to do? Remember, as I mentioned in chapter 2, the feminine heart wants to be a part of something larger than herself. A woman is looking to be fulfilled by committing her creativity to accomplishing a greater good.

"Then Jacob Kissed Rachel . . ." (Genesis 29:11)

The way Jacob kissed Rachel was very significant. In their culture, the way a person was kissed conveyed a specific message. If you kissed someone on the cheek, it was a kiss of cordiality. It was a standard greeting and an acceptable way to say hello. A kiss symbolized friendship and fellowship. This custom was encouraged by the apostles Paul and Peter in the New Testament with the admonition, "Greet one another with a holy kiss" (Romans 16:16).

Kissing on the lips was always a sign of affection. This possibly could have been going on in Genesis 26:8

when Abimelech realized Rebekah was Isaac's wife and not his sister. The Bible says, "It came to pass when he had been there a long time, that Abimelech king of the Philistines looked out at a window, and saw, and, behold, Isaac was sporting with Rebekah his wife."

Kissing someone's feet was a demonstration of submission, an inferior to a superior, as in the case of subjects to kings. In fact, a king who won a war would have his feet kissed by the defeated king. The victor would then place his feet on the head of the defeated king.

It was typical for a blessing to be bestowed with a kiss on the forehead.

When Jacob kisses Rachel's hand, he is doing something countercultural. It was commonplace for a woman to kiss a man's hand, but a man would never kiss a woman's hand! A kiss on the hand was a sign of respect and admiration. In those days men didn't have much respect or admiration for women. Jewish men frequently prayed thanking God that they were not born women. By kissing her hand, Jacob was saying, "Rachel, I admire you."

What was there to admire so early in the relationship? Jacob was impressed and expressed admiration for Rachel's willingness to do what a man was supposed to do without murmuring or complaining about the work.

In contemporary terms, Jacob may express to a single mother, "I admire you! Your husband has abandoned you and left you with three children to raise all by yourself. Yet, you raised them, put them through college, and they have grown up to become respectable, contributing members of society. Please, let me do something men don't usually do. Please allow me to kiss your hand, because I appreciate and admire your diligence." When Jacob kissed Rachel's hand, he conveyed his appreciation, which affirmed her activity.

Listen, married men. You need to kiss your wife's hand! Does she know how much you admire her vocation? Her appearance? Her contributions to your success? If she wears her hair to one side, you ought to notice and tell her how wonderful she looks: "I notice everything about you. You got your eyebrows arched too, didn't you? Looks good on you, girl! Kinda sexy." Then when she starts walking away: "Girl, you walkin'. You walkin', girl. Lord, have mercy, Jesus! I give in! I give up! I surrender ALL! Lookin' good, girl! You GO!"

She needs that kind of admiration, and not just in regard to her physical appearance. A woman needs spiritual, social, and intellectual affirmation. She needs to know that you care about her and appreciate her as a person. The woman in Proverbs 31 is special, isn't she? Well, she still exists today. God doesn't put a model before you that does not exist. If you believe that your woman has a ways to go to live up to the standard, then speak what you want to see into existence! Remember: "Death and life are in the power of the tongue: and they that love it shall eat the fruit thereof" (Proverbs 18:21).

Proverbs 31:28 tells us that the children of the virtuous woman rise up and call her blessed. Let me tell you what her kids do. Her kids get up in the morning and say, "Ooh, Mama! You have breakfast on the table again. Thank you. Ooh, Mama, you have lunch for us today. Thank you! Thank you for putting money in our pockets and taking us to school and to our friends' homes. We are so glad we can bring our friends to a clean house. A lot of my friends come to school dirty. I have clean clothes. Sometimes my friends don't have food. I always do. Sometimes they go home and are all alone. They have no one to talk to or to help them with their homework, but I do! Thank you, Mama." That is what her children say!

Proverbs 31:28 continues to say that the husband of the virtuous woman praises her. Here's what motivated her, what kept her going: the praise and encouragement of her husband. Her husband said, "You go, girl! Look at you. A regu-lar little bid-nez woman. Doin' your bid-nez on the side. Doin' your thang in the house. Got your bid-nez, takin' care of the kids, keepin' the house clean . . . You got it goin' on! Oh, girl, I *knew* I had somethin' special when I got you . . ."

All of a sudden she feels the anointing to cook a good meal. All of a sudden she feels led by the Spirit to do the ironing. She gets gumption for dishwashing. Why? You praised her! Husbands, try to lift up your wives and tell them what you like about them, and I guarantee it will start turning—you will begin to see the things you desire to see. You will wonder what in the world is happening. You are letting her know that she is important to you. You are affirming her activity.

In fact, the statement in Proverbs 31:28 about her children rising up and calling her blessed also says that her husband praises her. Both statements are present tense. "Rise up" and "praise" are also the tense of continuous action. In other words, this was not a rare statement made after consuming an exquisite Thanksgiving meal. No! This was an ongoing, regular occurrence. Her children and husband established a regular habit of telling their mother and wife how much they appreciated her.

AN ATTITUDE OF GRATITUDE

When was the last time you sat down and took your fiancée's or wife's hand, looked her in the eyes, lowered your voice two octaves, and told her what you appreciate about her?

Jacob's sensitivity to and comprehension of Rachel's vocation seems to be intuitive. That ought not discourage any man, because we can grow in our appreciation just like Adam did for Eve.

In Genesis 2:23 Adam named Eve "woman," which means "out of man." So he identified her by that which best represented him. In Genesis 3:20, he calls her "Eve," which means "mother of all living ones." Adam finally grows to appreciate Eve's distinctiveness apart from who he was. He recognized and acknowledged her uniqueness. Eve's distinctive design is a designation that celebrates how uniquely God created her.

Gratefulness Defined

Gratefulness means "letting others know by my words and actions how they have benefited my life." Etymologically, the central meaning of the word *gratefulness* is "to be pleased and make it known."

Three Aspects of Gratefulness

Adam learned it as a married man. Jacob exhibited it as a single man and was a good husband for Rachel, because what he needed in marriage he practiced before marriage. He knew how to appreciate a woman so he would have no problem appreciating a wife. After all, Rachel was a woman before she became a wife!

1. Realization.

We must be aware of the benefits we have received! Our natural tendency is to be constantly aware of the benefits we extend and take those extended to us for granted. The first significant aspect of gratefulness is

34

to maintain an awareness of the daily benefits we derive, versus being acutely alert only after experiencing a loss.

2. **Response.**

After we identify how we have been blessed, our realization requires a response. I shared in a previous chapter about the value of blessings and how to give them. Also, I gave details about an annual special day I set aside to honor Leslie.

3. **Responsibility.**

The most significant way to communicate gratitude to a benefactor is through our stewardship and generosity. "He who refreshes others will himself be refreshed" (Proverbs 11:25 NIV). The way we utilize the gifts given to us demonstrates the degree of our gratefulness.

The pioneer in discovering the impact of emotions on health, Dr. Hans Selye, concluded that vengeance and bitterness are the emotions most likely to elicit high stress levels in the human body, while gratitude is the single response most nourishing to good health.

Gratitude challenges us to keep our personal demands to a minimum and simplify our expectations of each other. Good character does not require that we allow our personal autonomy to be trampled underfoot. Wisdom and discernment help us moderate expectations and self-seeking behavior, but not at the expense of personal care and safety.

When a man loves a woman, he cultivates the vision and purpose for his life, so that he can help cultivate and refine the life purpose of his beloved. This will be accomplished through giving her love; accepting her help, insight, and advice; and expressing gratefulness for these. He will encourage her to grow in faith and to maximize her natural gifts and abilities.

Chapter Four

WHEN A MAN LOVES A WOMAN

He Wins Her with Attention That Assures Her Security

*W*hen a man loves a woman, he demonstrates his concern by making sure that she feels a sense of security. A man in love wants to make sure his woman has everything she needs to succeed and not struggle with anxiety.

CHARACTER FIRST

Loving Concern Anticipates Needs

I believe that the character a man needs in order to be a good husband should be evident before he becomes a husband. Jacob anticipated and was willing to meet Rachel's need for assistance with moving the stone blocking the entrance to the well, so it's pretty likely he demonstrated the same kind of care and anticipation for her as his wife.

As a single man, Jacob implemented a New Testament concept. First Timothy 5:8 (NKJV) states, "If anyone does not provide for his own, and especially for those of his household, he has denied the faith and is worse than an unbeliever."

Paul tells Timothy that a man should anticipate the needs of his family. If he is not anticipating the needs of his wife, a husband is not adequately caring for her. If a husband does not seek to meet her spiritual, emotional, social, and material needs, then his wife may second-guess her ability to please him, and she may experience an identity crisis. A woman may question her inherent value and begin to wonder, *Am I woman enough for him?*'

The Old Testament equivalent is in Genesis 22, where God revealed Himself to Abraham as Jehovah-Jireh. Basically, *Jireh* means "to provide." God knew that Abraham would need a lamb for a sacrifice, so God put *what* Abraham needed, *where* Abraham needed it, *when* he needed it!

When Abraham lifted up his arm to slay his only, long-awaited son in obedience, God stopped him from sacrificing Isaac, and immediately Abraham saw that God had anticipated his need. Abraham called God Jehovah-Jireh— "the God who sees before." God sees what you need, before you realize you need it. Then He places what you need where you need it and opens your eyes to it when you need it!

Abraham saw the provision of God—a ram caught by his horns in a nearby thicket. This is a profound statement, because Abraham didn't just see a sacrificial animal that would take Isaac's place. He saw how God would provide propitiation for our sins at Calvary! God gave Abraham a glimpse into the future of humanity and allowed him to see the ultimate sacrifice who would take away the sin of the world in the person of Jesus Christ.

John 8:56 says, "Your father Abraham rejoiced to see my day: *and he saw it,* and was glad" (italics mine).

Impotent Men

There is a stark contrast between Jacob's attitude toward Rachel and the attitudes of the other men present at the well. The other men were so lazy, they refused to move the stone to water their own sheep. Certainly, they would not exert any effort to move the stone for Rachel. In fact, the Scriptures indicate that this was their common practice. Even though it was past time to water the flocks, the other men were waiting for someone else to move the stone for them! "And he [Jacob] said, Lo, it is yet *high day,* neither is it time that the cattle should be gathered together: water ye the sheep, and go and feed them. And they said, We *cannot,* until all the flocks be gathered together and till they roll the stone away from the well's mouth; *then* we water the sheep" (italics mine). Genesis 29:7–8

The cattle should have been grazing, but they had not been watered, because the men wanted someone else to do it for them. Jacob does by himself what the other men refused to attempt to accomplish together as a group. In fact, they said the stone covering the well's mouth could not be moved. "We can't do it."

This type of neglect is a subtle form of hostility. It is hostile for us to presume that we are not responsible *to* each other *for* each other! The lack of concern within the body of Christ for those who are in need is not unlike the attitude Cain had when God inquired of him, "Where is Abel thy brother?" Cain responded, "Am I my brother's keeper?" God spends the balance of Scripture addressing that issue with a persistent, unequivocal, and resounding YES.

Unfortunately, the "let someone else do it" mind-set is still prevalent today. Because the body of Christ has assumed the position that someone else will do it, there are tremendous needs that go unmet within the body of Christ! Scores of single mothers and children are living without basic needs being met, and ex-prisoners are hindered from rehabilitation, for example, because we are waiting for someone else to do what each of us, as members of the body of Christ, has a mandate to do! Rather than camping on the insistence that we *can't,* the body of Christ, most especially men, need to insist, "If not me, then who? If not today, then when?"

From "Damsel in Distress" to "New-Millennium Woman"

The custom of the day was that the men watered their flocks and herds first, then the women watered their flocks. Jacob moved the stone and told Rachel to come water her father's flock. If Rachel were a woman of the new millennium, she might have refused Jacob's offer.

Surprisingly enough, there are women who feel demeaned when a man offers his seat to her or opens a car door and ushers her in first. These new-millennium women don't understand that to deny this kind of attention is to relinquish some of their femininity and diminish a man's masculinity. Ironically, Christian women frequently complain that their men will not assume leadership, yet they do subtle things to emasculate and feminize them!

Society has spent the last few decades redefining what it is to be masculine. Now masculinity is more safe and feminine. Yet, women consistently ask, "Where are all the *real* men?" We asked them to be women! Every man wants to play the hero and know that he is powerful.[11] Chivalry should be welcomed by women and encouraged, particularly if they want their men to be strong, assertive leaders.

Rachel readily received Jacob's gesture of care. She acknowledged that she needed help, and I'm sure she realized that a group of women couldn't assist her with this particular task, since there was a group of men present who found it daunting for their physical capabilities.

God wants us to be interdependent! That's why we are a body. For a woman to presume that she doesn't need a man, or vice versa, is the ultimate presumption! Further, our lives are out of balance if we don't have input from men and women. Jacob was able to help Rachel because he was sensitive to Rachel's need. Rachel was happy to receive his help, and I am sure that Jacob's behavior at the well distinguished him. Since Jacob was sensitive as a single man, it was likely that he would be sensitive as a married man and make a good husband.

When a Man Loves a Woman, He'll Give 100 Percent

Jacob was not a fifty-fifty kind of man, like some men who say, "She's got to meet me halfway." If a relationship is a fifty-fifty proposition, where do you draw the line? In other words, how do you know when you have fulfilled your 50 percent?

As a married man, I must admit that sometimes we say some pretty stupid things, like, "You pay this bill and I will pay another . . ." No! In the spirit of establishing a spirit of oneness, why don't we pool our resources and pay our bills together because we are one?

We can learn from Jacob that the man is the initiator in a love relationship, and the woman is the responder. As the thermostat, the man generally sets the climate for the relationship, and the woman usually registers it. Her very body, as discussed in the previous chapter, illustrates her posture to receive.

Rachel can be secure because she knows her needs will be anticipated and met. She is confident that she will get the attention that she desires and deserves, because when a man loves a woman, he will make her feel secure.

Chapter Five

WHEN A MAN LOVES A WOMAN

He Wins Her with Affection
That Affirms Her Femininity

> *Then Jacob kissed Rachel and began to weep*
> *aloud.*
>
> Genesis 29:11 NIV

I love you, not only for what you are,
but for what I am when I am with you.
I love you, not only for what you have made of yourself,
but for what you are making of me.
I love you for the part of me that you bring out.
I love you for putting your hand into my heaped-up heart
and passing over all the foolish, weak things that you can't
help dimly seeing there,
and for drawing out into the light all the beautiful belongings
that no one else had looked quite far enough to find.
I love you because you are helping me to make of
the lumber of my life not a tavern, but a temple,
out of the works of my every day not a reproach but a song. [12]

When a man loves a woman, he wins her with compassion. Notice verse eleven says Jacob "lifted up his voice, and wept." Jacob wins Rachel with compassion. He lifted up his voice and wept. This wasn't a silent sob. It was a soprano cry, not a bass one.

Wait a minute! This is powerful and virtually unheard of. A man who is not ashamed to cry in the open in front of a woman while other men are looking at him.

When I arrived at this point in the Scripture, I cried. Why did I cry, you ask? Well, I will tell you why.

I cried because I thought of the hundreds of couples I have counseled over the years. Frequently, I see women who have been verbally or physically mistreated by a husband who just sits there stoic, cold, and uncaring. He didn't want to come for counseling in the first place and had to be coerced, literally kicking and screaming the whole way. Then, when he gets to my office, everything is her fault, and he doesn't accept any responsibility for the current problems in the relationship. I have seen women literally get down on their knees begging their husbands to listen and consider their part, only to have the men turn a cold shoulder. So I weep for these women, because, as a pastor, it has been the hardest thing I have to see.

To see and to hear the lack of consideration and brutal unkindness in some of these men . . . They think a woman is some kind of plaything or a toy. It's in counseling sessions with this type of man that I get very angry. I know it is the Spirit of God that stops me from getting up and starting a fight.

Jacob would have never exhibited such a mean spirit to Rachel. Jacob's tears were tears of compassion and an overt demonstration of empathy and affection.

The Command "to Love"

Women need affection from their husbands. A woman needs her husband to love her. There aren't any scriptures that I am aware of that *command* a woman to love a man. Titus 2 says older women should teach the younger women *how* to love their husbands. Why does God command a man to love his wife, but doesn't command a woman to love her husband? Perhaps because women have a natural inclination to be loving. Men need to work at it!

Men often ask: "Why isn't she giving me the kind of love I want?" Perhaps because you are not invoking that privilege. I can guarantee that you are not making the right kind of investment if you are asking this question.

A woman is like a bank account. If you make a love deposit in her emotional bank account, she will accept it, allow your investment to accrue interest, and then give it back to you in greater measure than what you originally deposited.

Conversely, if you give her drama, then she will give drama back to you. That drama will be pressed down, shaken together, and run over in abundance. If you are taking a love check to her emotional bank and submitting it for cash without sufficient funds in the account, your check is going to receive a stamp that says "Insufficient Funds," because you cannot take out more than what you have deposited into the account. Yet, there are many of us trying to cash $100 checks when we only have a balance of $10, so to speak.

Affection Is the Demonstration of Compassion

Women want affection! Dr. Willard Harley, in his book *His Needs, Her Needs,* says that affection is a woman's number one need. He calls it "the first thing she can't do without."

To most women affection symbolizes security, protection, comfort, and approval. Affection is a vitally important commodity in the eyes of a woman. When a husband shows his wife affection, he sends these messages: I will take care of you and protect you. You are important to me.[13]

In fact, have you ever considered the power of a hug? Of course, a hug is just a little thing, but it is a powerful demonstration of affection. A hug says: I like touching you. You are very desirable to me. You are very important to me. I want to be close to you. I am proud of you. I want to protect you. We are one. I love you. I like taking care of you. I am on your side.

In the movie *Milk Money,* three twelve-year-old boys ask leading actress Melanie Griffith if there is a place on a girl's body where you can touch her and she will go crazy. In the beginning of the movie, she tells them no such spot exists. At the end of the movie, Ms. Griffith turns to the boys and says, "Hey, boys, there is a place you can touch a woman and drive her crazy. Right here," as she points to her heart.

Jacob knew that too! He knew that when a man loves a woman, he will know how to touch her heart with displays of compassion and affection!

Chapter Six

WHEN A MAN LOVES A WOMAN

He Establishes Companionship That Solidifies the Relationship

*A*llow me to reiterate. Everything Jacob needed to be *in* the marriage, he was *before* the marriage, even before he knew there was going to be a marriage. Jacob demonstrated these characteristics to this woman even before he was sure she would be his wife. He did it because he was a man of character.

WHEN A MAN LOVES A WOMAN, HE WILL TALK TO HER

In his book *Lonely Husbands, Lonely Wives*, Dennis Rainey relates the following story:

> My daughter, Ashley, slipped into my study and asked me what I was writing about. "Isolation," I replied. "Do you know what that means?"

"Oh," said my blue-eyed, blonde-haired, freckle-faced 10-year-old *"that's when somebody excludes you,"* [italics mine].

I may be a bit prejudiced, but I like Ashley's answer better than the dictionary's definition, which says isolation is "the condition of being alone, separated, solitary, set apart."

I think Ashley's definition is profoundly accurate too. When you are excluded, you have a feeling of distance. There is a lack of intimacy and closeness. What makes isolation and exclusion especially devastating, though, is the idea that there is a person or persons who intentionally, with forethought, want to make you feel alone! Not only are they not concerned about your solitude, but they want you to experience it. They are cruel and calculating in their exclusion. You may have sex, but you don't have love; you may live together, but you don't share life and common interests. You may talk, but you don't communicate.

WHEN A MAN LOVES A WOMAN, HE WILL WIN HER WITH CONVERSATION

Notice what it says in verse 12 of our text: "And Jacob *told* Rachel that he was her father's brother, and that he was Rebekah's son" (italics mine). The word *told* needs to be explained. To tell means to relate in detail, communicating knowledge. Synonyms of *told* include *inform, relate* and most interesting, *affirm*. According to *Funk and Wagnall's New Practical Standard Dictionary,* to *tell* is synonymous with *affirmation!*

Jacob is giving Rachel more than information. He is giving Rachel affirmation.

Elements of Affirming Communication

Affirming communication avoids *prideful presumption*. The Hebrew word for *presumption* describes a person who has an exaggerated sense of self, who assumes more authority than he has been given. A presumptuous person believes he is entitled to things which do not belong to him. He ventures into areas that go beyond recognizable limits.

Affirming communication is free from *scorn*. A scorner uses facial expressions to communicate disdain and contempt. He shows repugnance toward people and ideas that contradict his erroneous conclusions. Scorn is expressed in attitudes, behavior, and speech.

Affirming communication will also avoid any message that can create *disillusionment*. An illusion is an erroneous perception of reality. Thus, disillusionment means to destroy one's illusions. In other words, when a man loves a woman, he will communicate in sincerity, without expectation, being careful not to make promises he can't keep or create unrealistic expectations or false perceptions. He will just be "real."

In contrast, affirming communication comes from a heart that is wise, wholesome, encouraging, contrite, pure, and upright. A *wise* heart listens actively and eagerly receives. A *wholesome* heart is curative! It is not easily overthrown or turned. A heart full of *encouragement* knows how to calm fears, giving strength to the faint, and visualize circumstances and situations from God's perspective. A *contrite* heart is conscience-led and humbled, demonstrating a decreasing estimation of himself. John the Baptist exemplifies this when he concludes, "He must increase, but I must decrease" (John 3:30). A *pure* heart is singular. It involves transparency. A pure heart does not have conflicting motives or a hidden agenda. Finally, an *upright* heart describes a person who is reliable and has integrity. David resolved: "I will behave myself wisely in a perfect way. . . . I will walk within my house with a perfect heart" (Psalm 101:2).

Nonverbal Communication

There are three elements of communication. Not only do we convey our thoughts with words, but rhetoricians (those skilled in the use of language to persuade) tell us that when you speak, 50 percent of what you communicate is declared by your tone, 30 percent by your body language, with only 20 percent of how you feel actually communicated by your words.

For example, my wife says, "Honey, will you take out the garbage?" and I say, "Yeah," in a sarcastic tone. Her response is, "No. Don't take it out." Then I say, "Well, I said yeah." Next there is an explosion.

"Now why are you getting an attitude, huh? You asked me to take the garbage out. I'm getting ready to take the garbage out. Why are you getting an attitude, huh? You know I don't like the way . . ."

Wait a minute. Didn't I say yeah? I said yes, but my body language and my tone said no.

Things usually escalate from there, don't they? My wife concludes, "OK, you don't want to take out the garbage. That's all right. I'll let you know there are plenty of men who want to take my garbage out."

Now, you know I don't like that, so I respond, "Well, you better go ahead and call one." The fight really starts when she walks toward the phone!

Jacob understands that when a man loves a woman, he will talk to her. He will communicate with her. Why?

Jacob realizes that intimacy is created and solidified through communication. Soul ties are formed through words. Words heal (Proverbs 12:18). They can promote understanding when the speaker forgoes a determination to be right (Proverbs 18:2). They convey acceptance (Proverbs 10:32).

Women Are Verbal, and Intimacy Is Built Through Communication

All you have to do is look at your phone bill to know that women are verbal creatures! Now, I know there are exceptions to the rule, but in general this is the case. Jacob knew that if he wanted to win Rachel's heart, he would have to talk to her.

You Don't Talk to Me!

If you are having problems in your relationship because your wife says, "You don't talk to me," what is she really saying? You don't talk to her! You wonder, *Where is this coming from?* Well, it's coming from the amount of time and attention you spent talking with her prior to getting married, as compared to how much you talk with her now.

Look, brothers, you have to rap, and you ought to know it by now! How did you win her? You talked. You told her how much you loved her. You commented on everything. You said this. You said that . . . You must continue to do that.

It's like the story of the man who had been married for forty years. His wife asked, "Do you love me?"

He said, "Look, honey. I told you forty years ago that I love you. If I change my mind, you'll be the first to know."

My wife can tell me once a year, "I love you." That's good enough for me. She told me last year she loved me. She said it again this year, but she really didn't need to. I speak to her every day, and every day guess what I say. "I love you, Leslie." Doesn't she know that? Of course! There are exceptions to every rule, but by and large, women appreciate affirmation because it creates a sense of security for the present. Yes, I said "I love you" yesterday, but she needs a reaffirmation of that fact today. I have to do it. You have to do it, and you must keep doing it. This is especially important during the summertime when it's hot and some women are not as modest as they should be—know what I'm sayin'? You must reaffirm your wife and reassure her that she's the only one for you. "There's no one else for me, and I want you to know that."

She thought that communication between the two of you would increase once you were living together, not decrease. You don't talk as much as you did before you won her. You've cut off communication, and you're wondering why she's like she is? Because she still desires and needs conversation with you. Follow these principles to become more effective in your communication:

1. Initiate conversation. This communicates "I like talking to you."

2. Get rid of distractions. Turn off the television to convey "You are important to me, more important than what I am currently doing."

3. Make eye contact to show you are receptive to what's being said.

4. Wear a pleasant expression. Your face will communicate that you are enjoying the conversation.

5. Use vocal clutter to show that you are listening and empathize.

6. Use appropriate touching. If you touch her face while

she is talking, you are telling her that you love her. If you take her hand, you communicate sympathy and sensitivity to her feelings. An arm around her says, "I will protect you."

7. Give an affirmative conclusion. This is where you convey that if things are not resolved, you are open to listening whenever she feels the need to discuss the issue again.

Women Believe That Questions Are Synonymous with Caring

Women ask lots of questions. When men ask questions, it's for the purpose of gathering information or in an attempt to solve a problem. Women ask questions to carry on a conversation. Let me set the scenario:

"Baby, what did you do today? What happened in your ministry?"

"Uh, nothing."

"Well, what was the nothing you did all day?"

"Uh, I talked to this person, that person."

"Well, what happened?"

"Nothing . . . you know."

"What did you do for lunch?"

"Ate."

"Where did you go afterward?"

"Somewhere with somebody."

Here's what's happening. He's thinking, *Why is she asking all these questions? I'm a grown man. She's trying to check up on me. She wants to know too much. Why's she got to know all that?*

Because she is trying to create an atmosphere of intimacy, and that is done through conversation. You have been apart for eight to ten hours, and your worlds have not merged. Now she wants to be brought into your world. The only way that can happen is if you tell her what happened in your world so that she can feel a part of it and who you are.

A woman thinks, *If I don't ask, he'll think I don't care.* That's why women ask lots of questions. I'm telling you, brothers, the number one reason women ask is because they care about you.

By and large, questions for men represent meddling. Women, on the other hand, use them to express caring. To flip the script: If you come home after work and don't ask about her day, what you have communicated by not opening your mouth is "I don't care about what you went through today. It really doesn't matter to me. I'm not concerned. You probably didn't do anything important anyway . . . It doesn't matter because I didn't ask you."

Understanding the Way Your Partner Communicates

My wife would say, "James, I need to tell you something that is very important. This is going on . . ." I would look her dead in the eye. I wouldn't look left or right. She would say, "You are not listening to me."

I would say, "Wow. Baby, I'm standing right here looking you eye to eye. What in the world? Why would you say I'm not listening and that I don't care?"

"You don't," Leslie would respond. "You're looking at me, but your mind is a thousand miles away. I can see through your empty eyes right to your brain. You're just staring off into space."

Yet, I would be paying full attention. She thinks I'm not listening because I am not interacting in a way that a woman converses. I'm not saying, "Uh-huh. Whoa! Yeah."

When two women talk, they show interest with lots of interjections:

"Yeah. What happened next, girl? . . . For reaaa-al?
. . ."

"Chile' pleeez . . . Uh-huh. Know you right, girl fren
. . ."

Now, when two brothers talk, things are pretty cut-and- dried:

"Yeah, man, xyz . . ."

"That's it?"

"Yeah. End of story."

I decided that when Leslie related a story to me, I would say, "Yeah, girl. Um-hmm. Lord have mercy, Jesus!" When I first started that practice, she told me, "You better quit pickin' at me, James!" Now she continues with the story, because I continued to interject and proved to her that I was expressing genuine interest in what she had to say. Today when she says, "So and so . . ." and I say, "Help me now, somebody!" Leslie doesn't take a break and proceeds with her story.

Women Have a Unique Perspective

There is another difference in the way women communicate that is very profound, significant, and important to understand. Unfortunately, most men do not realize this difference or value how helpful these differing perspectives can be in decision making when given just regard to their proportional relevance or importance. In addition, to value each of these perspectives and be committed to attentive listening further communicates security to a woman.

The four points of view or perspective that a woman will communicate from are intellectual, emotional, volitional, and spiritual. A response from an *intellectual* perspective will say, "That makes sense. I think it's a good idea." *Emotion* will say "I feel very uneasy about this decision. I don't feel good about this. I have a 'feeling . . .'" A *volitional* insight will say, "I have decided to allow you to make this decision, or I have decided that you have done more research in this area than I have, or I have decided that I am right about this." Communicating from a *spiritual* perspective may include her giving you scripture references, interpreting a potential solution or pitfall based on biblical principles, or simply communicating, "I am sure that God is going to teach me/you/us important lessons through the resolution of this issue."

Most men become confused when women switch from one perspective to another. They don't understand that women use conversation as a catharsis, because even though there may be a point-in-time decision, women need their emotions to catch up with their will, or intellect.

That's why all of a sudden, weeks after the two of you have resolved an issue, she revisits it. You get mad because she's bringing it up. You think she's trying to put you down for past mistakes, when she really hadn't completely resolved things. Our guilt causes us to cut off further discussion. We need to go on and let women talk it through. When we refuse to do so, we ultimately prolong the drama.

God explains that "counsel in the heart of man [woman] is like deep water; but a man of understanding will draw it out" (Proverbs 20:5). Taking the time to patiently consider and think through the four perspectives your wife communicates from ensures that you can benefit from her unique ability to consider an issue from different angles. The most important benefits are that you will bolster her feelings of security, self-worth, intelligence, value, judgment, and significance. To neglect attentive listening is to reject her God-given role as helpmeet to you.

Likewise, ye husbands, dwell with them according to knowledge, giving honour unto the wife, as unto the weaker vessel, and as being heirs together of the grace of life; that your prayers be not hindered.

2 Peter 3:7

Chapter Seven

WHEN A MAN LOVES A WOMAN

He Will Work for Her

> *And Jacob served seven years for Rachel; and*
> *they seemed unto him but a few days, for the*
> *love he had to her.*
>
> Genesis 29:20

*W*hen a man loves a woman, he demonstrates it through a commitment to his work. Through his commitment, Jacob demonstrated that he knew how to provide for a wife. "And he said, Lo, it is yet high day, neither is it time that the cattle should be gathered together: water ye the sheep, and go and feed them. And they said, We cannot, until all the flocks be gathered together, and till they roll the stone from the well's mouth; then we water the sheep" (Genesis 29:7–8).

Who is Jacob talking to? He's speaking to some brothers sitting by the mouth of the well. I believe God mentions the men in this text to highlight and contrast Jacob's determination with the lack of initiative of the men sitting around convinced the task was too big for them. The brothers are at the well in the middle of the day. Jacob comes along and says, "Hey. What's up? Why are you lounging around, laying in the cut? Why are you standing on the corner? The sheep are here. The well is here. There's McDonald's across the street. Why don't you water the sheep so they can graze? Why don't you get a job?"

They replied, "We cannot."

"Well, why can't you?"

"Because we're waiting for somebody to move the stone and uncover the well. When the other brothers come and do that for us, then we will be able to water the cattle."

When Rachel comes to the well to water her father's flock, she sees this new guy, and he is taking the stone from the mouth of the well alone! I can imagine her saying, "Whoa! *Who* is that? Umm, chile', let me move this veil a little lower and see who that is . . . Look at the regulars, standing around the way they do every day. They have to wait on their boys since they don't have the courage to attack a big job alone. They can't do anything alone, which means I have to wait on them so that I can have a turn at the well. Look at that! This new man moved the stone cover all by himself. I don't know who he is, but I know he's not part of the regular crowd. Kinda strong too. Now that's a *real* man!"

When Jacob asked the men why they were standing around, they gave him excuse after excuse. Similar excuses are prevalent today. "I can't find a job." Well, you certainly can't find a job if you aren't getting up to go look for one. If you look for a job long enough and hard enough, you will find one. "It's institutional racism. Black men are castrated by society." I don't deny that, but if that is the general rule and a valid reason for your unemployment, then there isn't a brother who should have a job. Others say, "Well, you know, my daddy wasn't around to show me how to be a man." He's not around now. How did you eat today? Who feeds you now, your mother? "I was mistreated as a child." What does that have to do with your ability to eat today? Assuredly, God gives all of His children the grace to overcome anything in our past. The problem is we allow circumstances to circumvent us, and we resist the grace available to us.

Anyway, the men at the well made excuses while Jacob went to work and moved the stone all by himself. Then he watered Rachel's sheep. On a normal day, Rachel had to wait until all the men were finished watering their flocks before she had an opportunity to tend to her father's sheep.

Jacob distinguished himself from all the other brothers. I can imagine them saying, "Look at him showing off." Jacob knew something they didn't. Boys playfully wait around, while men get right to work.

A Reproof and Encouragement for the Mothers of Adult Adolescent Sons

Contemporary mothers have created some of today's catastrophes that married women are living with. You allowed your son to remain at your breast until he was thirty-five years old! . . . and you wonder why his wife is frustrated with him.

If you have the misfortune of parenting an "adolescent adult," it's not too late to urge him to grow up! Keep hope alive. Here's what you have to do. If you get up at six o'clock in the morning to go to work while he lies in bed, don't fret. You can help him change by changing your enabling behavior. If you get up at six, he gets up at six. If you leave at seven, he leaves at seven. When he leaves at seven, you tell him, "Stay out there until you find a job." Take his keys, because if you don't, he will go back to the house once he thinks you are gone.

The future wife of your son will thank you for helping him develop the character of Jacob and instilling in him the determination to find enough work to support his family, even if that means he has to work at McDonald's, Burger King, and Wendy's all at the same time.

Don't miss what Jacob is demonstrating that the other men are not able to say: "I know how to take care of a woman, Rachel. I have a commitment to work. I will work to provide for you. When other men stand around waiting for a handout and don't know what a W-2 or a 1099 is, I will work to take care of you."

WORKING WIVES

There are working wives who will not appreciate this, but I appeal to them to pay close attention and consider the following. When you attempt to carry the financial burden of your household, you deprive your husband of the opportunity to fulfill a significant part of his God-ordained purpose. Just as it was not Rachel's responsibility to move the stone from the mouth of the well, it is not your responsibility to be the primary breadwinner for a family. You rob yourself of one of the benefits of marriage, you deny the man the privilege and obligation of working to win you, and you interfere with a significant aspect of his establishing his identity and self-worth.

You may not agree with it, but it is my opinion that if your lifestyle takes two incomes and necessitates that your wife must work, then you need to begin downsizing. Look at people who sacrificed their relationships on the altar of materialism. Ask them if all the material wealth contributed to the well-being of their relationship or ushered the breakdown of their relationship. You should downsize your living until you're able to provide for primary needs from his income alone. A couple in the church that I pastor sold their five-bedroom house and bought a three-bedroom home, cut up their credit cards as they paid them off, and made the necessary adjustment to live off of his income. They are doing very well, and she's at home helping to raise their children.

Some of you may remember living in an apartment when you didn't have two nickels to rub together, but you were happy. Now you have all the things but no time for each other, because you forgot you were supposed to love people and use things, not love things and use people. Quit using your wife as a means to get more material things and end up coming out on the short end in your relationship with her and your children.

What are you saying, Pastor Ford? I'm saying if you're in a big house and you have a lot of bill pressures, sell it. Move to a smaller house, go back to an apartment, whatever you have to do to maintain healthy relationships with your wife and children. Don't allow the materialism of the world to take away from what God has ordained to happen within the confines of marriage.

A Man's Work Is an Important Element of His Fulfillment and Life Purpose

A man gets a sense of satisfaction and pleasure from his work and knowing that there are those who depend on him. So, suffice it to say that if you *do* everything and you *have* everything, what does that leave for him to provide? Why should he bother if you are self-sufficient?

"I have my own house and car. I don't need no man," you say. Perhaps that is part of the reason you don't have one with the character of Jacob, but instead you have one of those brothers who chose to sat and "wait it out" at the mouth of the well.

I am not suggesting that you cannot work. What I am

saying is that your job should not be necessary to meet the primary needs of the household. Allow your man to fulfill your economic expectation that your financial situation would improve with marriage. You rob yourself of this privilege when you pay for everything. You lower your potential for an increased standard of living when you get up and go to work every day and he's lying around, on his "rusty dusty" in bed—the bed you paid for, eating the food you bought, and watching your television! As a matter of fact, the truth is he's pimping you.

If a Wife Works Away from Home, Then Her *Husband* Must Share the Workload at Home

Now men, you can't expect a woman to work a full-time job outside the house, then come home and do a full-time job in the house. If she's going to work forty hours outside the home, quit expecting her to do everything in the home. If you want her to share in your financial responsibility, then you need to share in chores. Start doing some of the cooking and cleaning. You cry, "I don't know how to do it." Well, she had to learn. You can learn too. Get her to teach you how to do laundry so you don't put colored clothes and white clothes together in hot water, for example.

Instead of coming home and waiting for something to be cooked for you, you do the cooking. It's easy. If you're going to have spaghetti, go to your local grocery store. You've seen them. Buy some spaghetti, probably "No. 8." When you get home, all you have to do is get a pot. Fill it with water. Turn on the stove. Place the pot on the stove and let the water boil. Put some oil (cooking oil, men. It will most likely be in the kitchen, not the garage!) in the water so that the spaghetti doesn't stick together. Place a pound of spaghetti in the water.

Let it boil. Test the spaghetti with a fork. If it's real hard, it isn't ready yet. Don't let it get too soft either.

Next, get a frying pan. Put it on the stove. Turn the stove on. Put some salt in the bottom of the frying pan. Now you are going to brown the ground beef, turkey, or chicken that you purchased at the store when you bought your spaghetti. Place it in the heated skillet. How do you brown it, you wonder? Just keep turning it until it turns from red to brown. Then you get some Prego or Ragu and you pour the oil off your browned meat. Let me say it again. Pour the oil off of the browned meat in the skillet. Take a sieve. Remove the spaghetti from the pot, pour it in the sieve, let the water run off. Combine the spaghetti, meat, and the sauce and stir. The spaghetti is finished.

Now, get a head of lettuce. Cut it up. Cut and combine tomatoes, a bell pepper, and maybe some mushrooms. Place all the salad fixings in a large bowl. Mix. Get some Italian bread. Cut it in half. Spread butter and sprinkle garlic powder on the bread. Warm it in the oven on broil until the top turns light brown. Voilá, dinner!

Within the recesses of every woman's heart, there are two voids. One of them can only be filled with Jesus Christ. The other can only be satisfied by a man, whose sole purpose is to make her the happiest woman in the world. A man's commitment to work communicates affirmation to a woman. Jacob's actions say, "You are a woman, Rachel, and you should not have to tend sheep. The other men may refuse to acknowledge it, but I realize that this is a man's job. I want to affirm your identity as a woman. Please, allow me to help you."

Now it is clear that God placed those guys that lacked initiative around the well to highlight and contrast Jacob's initiative and commitment to work. While the other guys were waiting for *someone* to do *something*,

Jacob knew that when a man loves a woman, he is always willing to take the initiative to meet her needs. Always.

Chapter Eight

WHEN A MAN LOVES A WOMAN
He Wants Only Her

> *Many waters cannot quench love, nor will*
> *rivers overflow it; if a man were to give all the*
> *riches of his house for love, it would be utterly*
> *despised.*
>
> > *Song of Solomon 8:7* NASB

Often, marrieds will look at a single person and wonder, *Why isn't she/he married?* Some singles look at married people and wonder, *Why are they married?* It is better to be single and wish you were married, than to be married and wish you were single! In the first situation, there is reason to hope. The second scenario is a living Hades.

What happens to marriages that cause couples to wish they were single and not want each other anymore? After much contemplation, I suggest that the following issues are some of the primary reasons couples long to be singles again:

1. I attained the goal. I don't have to work hard to win you.

2. The masks are off. Now we see each other as we really are versus the people we saw when we were dating.

3. We have both grown tired of being people we are not. The facade we were comfortable with before marriage is burdensome now.

4. Reality sets in. Love is enough to start a relationship, but it takes much more to sustain one.

5. Now we are living together.

6. We want something to change now that we are married that we were content to keep quiet about before we were married!

7. We used to do certain things before marriage that pleased our mate, but stopped doing them after marriage.

8. We are not as open to being corrected as we were before we were married.

9. Some things about marriage we simply did not know.

This list is by no means exhaustive, but it does give some insight into why couples end up saying, "I want a divorce!"

Jacob never had this problem with Rachel. He always had eyes only for her, even though he had another wife, Leah. "And he went in also unto Rachel, and he loved also Rachel more than Leah, and served with him [Laban] yet seven other years" (Genesis 29:30).

Why was Leah rejected? It is not Jacob's fault. It's Laban's fault. Leah's father pushed her on a man that never really wanted her. Jacob never loved Leah. Leah's father insisted that Jacob accept her in order to receive his true love, Rachel. That's why Leah was "dogged-out."

When a man loves a woman, he doesn't want anyone else. Even though Jacob was stuck in a culture where he had to take Leah as his wife, he never acted as if he loved her. The text never tells us Jacob loved Leah. He didn't love her. He worked fourteen years and fourteen days for Rachel. That's who he loved. He wanted only her. Jacob was a one-woman man. No one else could fit the bill. Rachel met all his needs.

I have two brothers who are not saved. When one of them comes to visit us in Chicago, he likes to visit a club called the "50 Yard Line." One night I asked him how he enjoyed his evening. He exclaimed, "Oh man! It was smokin'. I had my choice of women! That place is a player's delight!"

I reminded him that anyone can have a lot of women, but it takes a real man to go the distance with one woman and be faithfully committed to her. I commend men who are faithful to their wives, especially in the day in which we live. This morally decadent contemporary culture makes an extra-marital affair easy.

Have you heard the story about the guy whose wife asked him if he would remarry if she died. He responded, "No. Oh no, of course not. No way."

She said, "Oh. You don't like being married?"

"Well, wait a minute. Yeah."

"So you wouldn't get married again?"

"Well, yeah, I guess so. Yeah. OK. I'll get married again. After all, I do enjoy being married."

"Would you let her live in my house?"

"Well, yeah."

"You *would?* Would you bring her into our bedroom?"

"Yeah."

"You'd take my pictures out of the frame and put her up?"

"Yeah."

"You *would?* You'd let her use my golf clubs?"

"No. She's left-handed."

That's a funny vignette, but Jacob would not tease in that way. He never considered a life without Rachel. I told Leslie that if she ever leaves me, I'm going with her! One day in the middle of a heated argument, she started packing her suitcases. "I'm leaving," she bellowed.

I grabbed my suitcase and started packing and said, "I'm leaving too! Where are we going?"

No wonder Leah was jealous. She wanted what Jacob could only give to Rachel. When a man loves a woman, he wants her and no one but her.

Jacob was an "eagle" man! The American bald eagle is a one-eagle man for a lifetime. He is totally committed to one female eagle his entire lifetime. If his mate dies, he never hooks up with another female eagle.

God has Moses, the writer of the book of Genesis, to give glowing testimony to the commitment that Jacob has to Rachel. Genesis 46 lists all of Jacob's family who went to Egypt. Verse 15 lists the sons of Leah and verse 19 lists the sons of Rachel. Yet even though Leah was the first one married to Jacob, she was not called his wife. But verse 19 states "the sons of *Jacob's wife*" (italics mine).

What a tribute to Jacob's commitment. Rachel is the only one recognized as his woman. He's committed to her. He wants her and no one but her.

Chapter Nine

WHEN A MAN LOVES A WOMAN

He Will Wait for Her

Deacon Curtis Thomas informed me that two of our singles were living together. He went to make a home visit and saw both of their names on the mailbox. When he inquired, they replied that they were indeed "shacking." Deacon Thomas shared what the Scriptures say about such an arrangement, only to be told it was not his business.

At South Shore we practice church discipline and inform every person who attends our new members class about our accountability to each other spiritually, morally, and socially. Deacon Thomas explained that our church constitution and bylaws required him to share the situation with me. The man's response was that his living situation was none of my business either.

I followed up with a call and then a visit. The couple informed me that it was a matter of finances. I informed them that it was a matter of integrity. They were to be married in four months, so their "arrangement" would not be an issue much longer. I explained that four months is too long to bring reproach on the name of Jesus Christ. I extended the offer the church board empowered me to extend, which included helping the man find other housing if he would move out until they were married. He refused, and she went along with his decision.

My parting admonition was to the wife-to-be. If he is not disciplined enough to wait until marriage to have sex, he won't be disciplined enough to abstain from finding sex elsewhere in the future, if for some reason you are unable to be intimate during the marriage.

Of course, they left the church and vowed never to return to such a "pharisaical church." Just a short nine months later, the wife attended one of our services. I was quite surprised to see her and wanted to talk with her, but she left immediately after the service.

One of our head ushers, Mother Lampkin, came to me with a message from the wife. "Tell Pastor Ford he was right! We got married. Three months later I became ill and could not have sex. My husband divorced me two months later, and now he's living with another woman! He told me he could not live with me if I was unable to meet his sexual needs."

Don't Jump the Fence!

There is a fence around marriage called sex. If you won't stay outside the fence before marriage, you won't stay inside the fence after marriage. Don't jump the fence. God placed it there to protect, not punish you. Don't jump the fence! When a man loves a woman, he waits.

Notice what it says in verses 20 and 21. "And Jacob served seven years for Rachel; and they seemed unto him but a few days, for the love he had to her. And Jacob said unto Laban, Give me my wife, for my days are fulfilled, that I may go in unto her."

Jacob waited seven years and seven days. You know what his example teaches you? As Diana Ross sings, love isn't easy, and it can't be hurried. No matter how long, you have to wait. You just have to wait. One man said, "If you sit on the eye of a stove, one minute seems like one hour. But if a pretty girl is sitting on your lap, one hour seems like one minute." Time becomes relative. Notice what the Scripture says: to Jacob it seemed as if it was just a few days.

Now, you need to see the full picture. First, Rachel always wore a veil. The only thing Jacob ever saw was her eyes. Second, Jacob didn't know the shape of Rachel's frame, because women in Rachel's day did not wear belts around their waists. Their clothing was full, not at all formfitting, but like a tent.

For seven years Jacob is on his way out to take the sheep to pasture. He goes by Rachel's tent. She loves him and he loves her.

"Jacob?"

"Hey, girl, what's going on? How you doing? Six years left to go. I'll be coming to see you."

Think about the discipline required of Jacob. He never put his hands on her, because it was against the culture for a man to touch a woman, even to hold her hand unless she was his wife. He never kissed her, and he sure never put his tongue in her mouth! He never saw any part of her body except her eyes, because her face was veiled, and we'll talk about what that means in just a moment. Do you see the implication? Think that's hard on a brother? Here she is, eyes flashing. Every morning you're going out, coming in.

"Jacob? Jacob?"

"Five more years, girl. Three more years, girl. One more year, girl. Yeah."

He's willing to wait. You know how we say it's hard to wait? You know how we are chomping at the bit? Some of you engaged people know how hard you had to fight to keep from falling into immorality. Sometimes we get in these conversations. "You know, but we're going to get married anyway. . . . I know—but, I mean, the Lord will forgive us, you know? Because we're on our way there now, you know? . . . It's just so hard to wait."

Jacob said it just seemed like a few days. It really wasn't hard. Do you want to know why? Love is patient. Love knows how to put on the brakes. Love knows how to wait. In other words, when a man loves a woman, he's willing to wait until after they get married to live together and have sex.

Amnon was a man who found it hard to wait. In 2 Samuel 13:1–16, Scripture tells us:

> *And it came to pass after this, that Absalom the son of David had a fair sister, whose name was Tamar; and Amnon the son of David loved her. And Amnon was so vexed, that he fell sick for his sister Tamar; for she was a virgin; and Amnon thought it hard for him to do anything to her. . . . And he said unto him, Why art thou, being the king's son, lean from day to day? wilt thou not tell me? And Amnon said unto him, I love Tamar, my brother Absalom's sister. And Jonadab said unto him, Lay thee down on thy bed, and make thyself sick: and when thy father cometh to see thee, say unto him, I pray thee, let my sister Tamar come, and give me meat, and dress the meat in my sight, that I may see it, and eat it at her hand. So Amnon*

lay down, and made himself sick: and when the king was come to see him, Amnon said unto the king, I pray thee, let Tamar my sister come, and make me a couple of cakes in my sight, that I may eat at her hand. Then David sent home to Tamar, saying, Go now to thy brother Amnon's house, and dress him meat. So Tamar went to her brother Amnon's house; and he was laid down. And she took flour, and kneaded it, and made cakes in his sight, and did bake the cakes. . . . And she answered him, Nay, my brother, do not force me; for no such thing ought to be done in Israel: do not thou this folly. And I, whither shall I cause my shame to go? and as for thee, thou shalt be as one of the fools in Israel. Now therefore, I pray thee, speak unto the king; for he will not withhold me from thee. Howbeit he would not hearken unto her voice: but, being stronger than she, forced her, and lay with her. Then Amnon hated her exceedingly; so that the hatred wherewith he hated her was greater than the love wherewith he had loved her. And Amnon said unto her, Arise, be gone. And she said unto him, There is no cause: this evil in sending me away is greater than the other that thou didst unto me. But he would not hearken unto her.

Is It Love or Lust?

Amnon couldn't wait! He wanted to have sex with his sister Tamar, and his desire was so intense that it made him physically ill. Yet, the text says that he "loved" her. Actually, he lusted after her. What is the difference between love and lust? Love will wait, because it is patient. Second Samuel 13 helps us identify the characteristics of lust that won't wait. It is lust when

1. Objectivity is lost (verse 1). Wanting is based on the superficial, how Tamar looked outwardly and not how she was inwardly. His wanting is based on her physical appearance, not her personality.

2. Feelings override common sense and take control (verse 2). He literally got sick.

3. You are not concerned with the facts and will not respect the boundaries. Tamar is his sister (verse 2)!

4. You are in a hurry. Amnon was vexed (verse 2).

5. You will connive to get what you want. His cousin gave Amnon a scheme to utilize to get what he wanted (verses 4–6).

6. You will use whoever is necessary to get what you want. Amnon uses his father's influence (verse 7).

7. You use false pretenses and give into your emotions. Amnon got in bed as if he was sick, and he manipulated Tamar into baking a cake for him (verses 7–8).

8. You have a one-track mind (verse 14).

9. When satisfaction is gained, you want nothing else to do with the other person. Amnon rapes Tamar and then puts her out (verse 15b).

10. Contempt sets in (verses 15–16).

11. You will not listen to reason (verse 16).

Unlike Amnon, Jacob was a man who understood that when a man loves a woman, he will wait on her. Look at what the Bible says. Jacob waited patiently. He wasn't worried about time; he was worried about his testimony. He wasn't worried about resources; he was worried about Rachel's reputation. He waited patiently.

When I facilitate marriage seminars, one of the things I tell the brothers is that you are going to have to learn to wait on your wives. OK, I'm hungry. She has been upstairs getting ready for forty-five minutes. "Baby," I call, "how long are you going to be?"

"Two minutes," she replies. Now I want to interpret that for you, gentlemen. A woman's two minutes are equal to the two minutes that we tell them are left in the game that we're watching. Don't count the time-outs or the commercials. When we tell her there are only two minutes left in the game, we know that there is at least a half hour left!

Here is a secret I learned a few years back. When I ask, "How long are you going to be, because it's time to go?" and she says, "two minutes," I sit down, turn on the television, and get a cup of coffee, a Coke, and a smile or something! Then I wait. After a half hour, I walk to the top of the steps. I say, "Ooh, girl. You know I was sitting there hungry and I was worried about eating and about how long you were taking. But, girl, let me tell you something. Now that I look at you, it was worth the wait. I'll wait another half hour for you!"

I have learned how to wait!

Why Love Waits

Notice verse 21. Jacob waited for sexual involvement. It says, "Jacob said unto Laban, Give me my wife, for my days are fulfilled, that I may go in unto her." Jacob is saying, "I have done everything I was supposed to do, and now it is time to consummate the relationship." He waits until they're married before he expects to have sex. Let me say it again. He waits until they're married before he expects to have sex.

There are about forty-two reasons that Scripture gives to justify waiting to have sex until you are married. I am only going to highlight a few:

1. God commands us to be pure: 1 Thessalonians 4:2–5.

2. Premarital sex can make future courtship much more difficult: Proverbs 5–6.

3. Failing to wait strains freedom to develop strong relationships.

4. Premarital sex brings the risk of sexually transmitted diseases.

5. Premarital sex breaks your fellowship with God.

6. It can destroy self-esteem.

7. It creates problems in marriage.

8. It can produce unplanned pregnancies.

9. Premarital sexual relationships make it difficult to break up because you have had sex.

10. Sex, not love, is the basis for the relationship.

11. It causes guilt, guilt, and more guilt.

12. It will be subject to God's judgment.

13. The divorce rate is higher in marriages where there has been premarital sex than in marriages where both parties abstained.

14. Waiting brings the blessings of God.

15. Premarital sex generally leads to extramarital affairs.

16. It is a sin against your body.

17. It is a poor testimony.

18. It affects all society.

So when a man loves a woman, he will wait. He will wait for sexual involvement. Also, in verses 23 through 27, when a man loves a woman, he will patiently solve issues. This is really powerful! Here is the scenario (now tell me this is not better than a soap opera): A guy works for seven years for a woman. On his wedding night he consummates the marriage and wakes up the next morning, only to find out that it is not the woman that he thought he wed! He goes to the father and says, "You tricked me!" The father admits his deception, but claims there is a good reason, and he wants Jacob to work an additional seven years for his intended, Rachel!

Now Jacob has two wives and has worked fourteen years and fourteen days! Let's tell the truth. The average brother would have just shot the daddy. But no, Jacob said, "I am going to wait for Rachel." Could Jacob have insisted and said, "I don't want your other daughter. Give me my wife right now"? It might have cost him his life, but he could have made such a demand. Look at what Jacob did instead. He said, "There are some difficulties we have to work through, Rachel. I will wait and work through these issues, because I love you."

You say, "Make it practical." OK, I will!

You want to get married now. You have finished school and started a new job. Your fiancée still has three more years of college. Can you wait until she finishes school so that she might complete some of her educational goals?

The Mills of God Grind Slowly; They Grind Fine

The real essence of this story is that Jacob is going to reap what he's sown many years prior. Seven years before he met Rachel, Jacob tricked his blind father and his brother (Genesis 27–28:5). This present deception committed against Jacob by Laban may be a consequence of his earlier actions. No doubt Jacob learned that you may get by, but you don't get away. The mills of God grind slowly, but they grind fine.

Esau was planning a "drive-by" on Jacob, so his mother said, "Leave and go to my brother's house for a little while." "A little while" turned out to be twenty years, because sometimes when you plant something, the law of intensification says you always get more than what you plant. That's why the Bible says, "Sow the wind and reap the whirlwind (Hosea 8:7 NIV).

Furthermore, there's always someone a little slicker than you. Jacob was a manipulator and a deceiver. Jacob goes to his uncle Laban, who wrote the book on deception and manipulation.

Jacob, no doubt, understands how his brother, Esau, felt when he swindled him out of the firstborn's birthright, since Jacob inquires of Laban, "What is this that thou hast done unto me? did not I serve with thee for Rachel? wherefore then hast thou beguiled me?" (Genesis 29:25). What is it that will keep us from doing what our "natural" inclination may be? Put the shoe on our foot. How does it feel?

Jacob pays the high price of low living. Jacob's earlier deception cost him twenty years of his life. Yet, with consequences closing in all around him, Jacob waits for Rachel. Jacob did not whine about the consequences or give up on his dream of a life with Rachel, because he knew that when a man loves a woman, he will wait for her.

When a Man Loves a Woman, He Will Suffer through Consequences of Past Sin

If a husband commits adultery, he has been the victimizer. He is the one that is wrong. No matter what the wife's problem is, the responsibility lies with her husband. Her reaction is a consequence of his misbehavior. If she starts to treat him poorly, the husband is the one who initiated the problem, so he must take responsibility and work it through until she no longer feels victimized and is able to extend trust again. How long does it take?

I attended a Moody Bible Institute Pastors' Conference where the instructor shared, "If you have been the perpetrator in an affair, you need to know that you can gauge about how long it will take your wife to forgive you by how long you were in the affair."

It seems to take a person at least as long to get over the pain as they were in the pain. That will give you brothers some idea to gauge about how rough and how long a ride you've got if you are working through this type of betrayal. It's our job if we've offended our wives in any way to go through the process of rebuilding trust and waiting patiently for them to extend it to us.

Chapter Ten

WHEN A MAN LOVES A WOMAN
He Works to Wed Her

$\mathcal{I}$n order to marry in Jacob's culture, you had to have
three things established before you even approached
your prospective wife's father. These are consistent with
the order God established with Adam. First, He gave
Adam work (Genesis 2:15). Second, God gave Adam
specific instructions on how to live in his world, and
finally God gave Adam a wife. I tell single women, if a
man doesn't have a job, don't marry him. If he has no
means to provide for himself, how can he provide for
her? In fact, I refuse to officiate at weddings if the man
does not have a job.

When a man loves a woman, he will work to be with
her. Notice what Genesis 29:15–18 says: "And Laban
said unto Jacob, Because thou art my brother, shouldest
thou therefore serve me for nought? Tell me, what shall
thy wages be? And Laban had two daughters: the name

of the elder was Leah, and the name of the younger was Rachel. Leah was tender eyed; but Rachel was beautiful and well favoured. And Jacob loved Rachel; and said, I will serve thee seven years for Rachel thy younger daughter."

Don't miss this! Laban is rich. I imagine in the vernacular of today Laban would ask, "What kind of salary do you want?" A typical contemporary young man may respond: "Well, give me $70,000 a year, a nice 401(k) plan. Profit sharing. I want a part in the business, a company car, and a private office."

That's not what Jacob said. "Give me Rachel. I want to work for Rachel's hand in marriage."

So he worked seven years for Rachel and seven years for Leah, right? No. He worked fourteen years for Rachel! The working that we looked at in chapter 7 was accomplished before Jacob got married. In that work he acknowledged Rachel as a woman and proved that he understood how to treat a lady. That took one afternoon.

Jacob is working to prove he's willing to make a life-long commitment. He has declared his love for Rachel and established a course to make her his wife. It required fourteen years—seven years before he could marry Rachel, and seven more years of working for Laban after marriage (Genesis 29:26–30). But for fourteen years he hung in there. Why? Because he wanted Rachel to be his wife.

A FATHER PROVIDES PROTECTION AND ACCOUNTABILITY

I want you to know that Jacob worked for her by working through. He worked through every requirement that Laban demanded of him. Don't miss this principle. Jacob was willing to deal with Rachel's daddy. I believe this with all my heart. A young woman who is on her way to be married ought to have passed her intended by her dad.

Ladies, please pay special attention to the text. It says at the end of verse 12, "And Jacob told Rachel that he was her father's brother, and that he was Rebekah's son." Rachel did not run and tell her girlfriends, or the people at church. She ran and told her father!

Let your father analyze any man who is trying to step to you. There is protection in this for you. Your dad isn't going to go for the things you see in a man. Your boyfriend is telling you how beautiful your eyes are . . . Your dad is going to look *him* dead in the eye and assess his character. Your father will perceive what kind of man he is.

The Father: Covenant Initiator

Men had to pay a dowry to marry. Actually, it was more than compensation to make up for the daughter's lost contribution to the household, since she would be working in her own household now. The primary purpose of the dowry was for the groom to demonstrate to his prospective in-laws his ability to care and provide for their daughter.

This practice still exists today in Ghana, West Africa. Pastor Raphael, whom I met on a missions trip, showed me his dowry list. He had to provide what was asked for by each member of his fiancée's family. I asked him how long he thought it would take to amass their requests. He told me approximately three years. Wow! He also told me that his in-laws would not permit the wedding to take place until he had provided *all* that was requested. In fulfilling the requests of his future family, Pastor Raphael demonstrated the value he placed on his future wife and reassured them that he would be capable of caring for their daughter.

This Western culture stuff has got to go. In the East you know the drill well. The marriage is established between the bride's father and the prospective groom. The two men get together. It has nothing to do with the woman, per se, because her father has the right before God to transfer authority over his daughter.

Johnny Lingo

I want to share with you the story of Johnny Lingo. Johnny Lingo lives in the southern islands. Years ago a man from America went to these islands. He wanted to get some trinkets, artifacts and all of that. So, he went to the village of Kenny Watti.

> I went to the island of Kenny Watti to seek out someone who would be a trader to help me get the things that I had on my list. I said, "Who's the best trader on the island?"
>
> With a smile on his face, one native said, "Without a doubt, Johnny Lingo. Johnny Lingo." And then he laughed.
>
> I said, "Well, why are you laughing when you say his name?"
>
> He says, "Everybody here does [laughs], because, you see, Johnny paid eight cows for his wife, Serita."
>
> "What? Eight cows? Well, I guess there's no accounting for love," I said.
>
> "True enough," agreed the man.
>
> And that's why the villagers grin when they talk about Johnny. They get special satisfaction from the fact that the sharpest trader in the islands was bested by Doll Old Sam Carew.
>
> "But how?" I inquired.
>
> "No one knows, and everybody wonders," he said.

All the cousins were urging Sam to ask for three cows and hold out for two until he was sure Johnny would pay only one. Then Johnny came to Sam Carew and said, "Father of Serita, I offer eight cows for your daughter."

"Eight cows," I murmured. I'd like to meet this Johnny Lingo. I wanted fish. I wanted pearls. So the next afternoon I beached my boat at Nurabundi, the island that Johnny lived on. I noticed as I asked directions to Johnny's house that his name did not bring the sly smile to the lips of his fellow Nurabundians as it did those on Kenny Watti. Then I met the slim, serious young man. He welcomed me with grace to his home. I was glad that from his own people he had respect unmingled with mockery.

We sat in his house and talked. Then he asked, "You come here from Kenny Watti?"

"Yes," I said.

"They speak of me on that island?" he asked.

"They said there's nothing that I might want that you can't help me get," I said.

He smiled gently. "My wife is from Kenny Watti."

"Uh, yes, I know," I said.

"They speak of her?" he asked.

"Uh, a little."

"Well, what do they say?"

"Why, just uh . . ." The question caught me off balance. "Uh, they told me you were married at festival time."

"Nothing more?" The curve of his eyebrows told me he knew there had to be more.

"Well, they also say that the marriage settlement was eight cows, and . . ." I paused.

"They wonder why? They asked that?" His eyes lighted with pleasure. Everyone in Kenny Watti knows about the eight cows."

I nodded, "Yes, they do."

He said, "Well, in Nurabundi everybody knows it too." His chest expanded with a satisfaction as he said, "Always and forever when they speak of marriage settlements, it will be remembered that Johnny Lingo paid eight cows for Serita."

So that's the answer, I thought. *Vanity. Pride.*

Then I saw her. I watched her enter the room to place flowers on the table. She stood still a moment to smile at the young man beside me. Then she went swiftly out again. She was the most beautiful woman I've ever seen in my life! The lift of her shoulders, the tilt of her chin, the sparkle of her eyes all spelled a pride to which no one could deny her the right. I turned back to Johnny Lingo and found him looking at me.

"You admire her," he murmured.

"She's glorious. But she can't be Serita from Kenny Watti," I said.

He said, "There's only one Serita. Perhaps she does not look the way they told you she looked in Kenny Watti. She doesn't."

"I'm sorry, but I heard she was homely. They all make fun of you because you let yourself be cheated by Sam Carew."

"Do you think eight cows was too much for that woman?" he asked, as a smile slid over his lips.

"No, but how can she be so different?"

"Do you ever think," he asked, "what it must mean to a woman to know that her husband has settled on the lowest price for which she can be bought? And then later when the women talk they boast of what their husbands paid for them. One says four cows, another maybe six. How does the woman feel, the woman who was sold for one or two? This could not happen to my Serita."

"Then you did this just to make her happy?"

"Yes. I wanted Serita to be happy, but I wanted more than that. You say she is different. That is true. Many things change a woman. Things that happen inside, things that happen outside. But the thing that matters most is what she thinks about herself. In Kenny Watti, Serita believed she was worth nothing, so she acted like nothing and she looked like nothing. Now she knows she is worth more than any other woman on every island."

"Then you wanted—" He cut me off.

"I wanted to marry Serita. I loved her and no other woman."

"But . . ." I interrupted. I was close to understanding.

"But," he finished softly, "I wanted an eight-cow wife."

Listen, this man working for this woman does not apply practically in our culture. We don't work for our women. But the principle is true and should be true in our culture as well.

What are you saying, Pastor? I'm saying that what this man did was prove to his bride how valuable she was to him before he got married. Also, he established that he was somebody that was worthy to be married.

What does a man communicate when he works for a woman? You are valuable. I want you to know that there's no other man who will value you above the way I value you. Therefore, if I have to deal with your family for fourteen years just to walk you down the aisle, I love you enough and value you enough and want to spend the rest of my life with you enough to work through and devote the time.

You see, what we need is individuals who will wait to marry until they can resolve problems that have the potential to shipwreck. If I have to deal with your family—perhaps they don't like me. I'll win your family in order to win you. If you've got problems because of a previous relationship you were in, we'll work through those. Perhaps you got dogged out and kicked to the curb; then I'll do whatever it takes to help you heal. We'll get counseling. We'll do whatever it takes. I want you to know how valuable you are to me. I'll work for you because I want an eight-cow wife.

Jacob worked fourteen years for Rachel because *he* wanted an eight-cow wife.

The Husband: Covenant Responder

Do you know why the groom's family sits on one side of the church and the bride's on the other at a wedding? This is to symbolize the covenant relationship that the couple, as well as their families, are about to enter into. In Jacob's day an animal would be slain, cut in half diagonally. The two halves would be separated and the covenant participants would walk in between the halves, stepping in the blood. In Genesis 15:9–17, this picture is given to Abraham. In this case the covenant was unconditional, because only YAHWEH walked through the sacrifice.

In marriage, the bride's father is the covenant initiator and the groom is the covenant responder. That is why the groom does not walk down the aisle. The father brings his daughter down the aisle because he is her authority. When the preacher asks, "Who gives this woman to this man?" and the father says, "I do," it symbolizes transference of authority. His daughter will no longer be under his authority, but under a new covenant authority, her husband. The first sign that the wife comprehends and accepts this is the voluntary acceptance of her husband's last name by adopting it as her own. ". . . God made he him; male and female created he them; and blessed them, and called *their* name Adam . . ." (Genesis 5:1–2 italics mine).

A Father Continues to Provide Accountability, Instruction, and Counsel

Before I was saved, I had a gambling problem. I used to leave work and go to Jimmy Giles, the local gambling house every Friday after I got paid. Sometimes I would lose all of my money; sometimes I would win. Some of you know what I mean. You are playing the lottery!

Anyway, I told my wife I would not gamble anymore. Yet there I was, sitting in the gambling house at three o'clock in the morning. Suddenly, there was a knock at the door. Jimmy Giles got his gun and went to the door. (It's a gambling house, so he got his gun, then went to the door!) Before I knew it, two big hands were resting on my shoulders, practically covering them. I looked up and said, "Hey pops," to my father-in-law who had just arrived.

He said, "Sonny Man," that's what he called me, "Sonny Man . . ."

Now you need to understand that I dated my wife for eight years before we got married. And in eight years I bet you my father-in-law had not said ten words to me, during the entire eight years! I heard that man talk more that evening than I had ever heard him talk.

"Sonny Man," he said, "my daughter is at home crying. Let's go."

I said, "Oh. Let me finish this hand."

"Let's go. If I tell you one more time, you're going to be sorry."

I said, "I got to go."

He started talking from the time I left my seat at the card table.

"My daughter is at home crying, and I'm going to tell you this, and you better listen to me." I was walking ahead of him more than an arm's length.

"Sonny Man," he continued, "if my daughter ever has to call me to get you again, we're going to find out how much man you really are."

When I got home, I put my key in the door and found my wife standing in the middle of the floor with my son crying.

We sat on the couch, and I shriveled up like a piece of bacon.

Her father said, "Baby, here he is. Now I'm going to let you two work this out. And, sweetheart, let me tell you something. If you need me, you got my number. If you ever have this situation again, you call me. He already knows what we're going to do about it."

If you ever meet my wife, ask her if I ever went back to Jimmy Giles or if I ever had a gambling problem after that night. I was "saved" before I got saved from gambling. Leslie's daddy scared the gambling out of me!

After the Ceremony

When a man loves a woman, he will work for her by working through, and he will work for her by working with. Jacob is not living in the same tent as Rachel right now. Everything that happens in Genesis 29 is from afar. When you look at chapter 30, verses 1 and 2, Jacob has joined his wife in the tent.

How many of you know that what you see is not always what you get? I like what Tony Evans says: "You don't know what you got before you get married and you go to Steak and Ale. You sit down, and you're looking across at each other. She's all made up. She's demure and petite, and she's talking real soft, and conversation is real good. That's not what you really got. That's not what you really have. See, once you get married, you'll find out what you really have."

Anybody that's married will tell you there's a honeymoon stage. That's when you can't keep your eyes off of each other. You can't keep your hands off of each other. Guess what. The honeymoon stage ends. When the honeymoon stage ends, the real work of marriage starts. Most people think they've been tricked. They've been hoodwinked. They've been bamboozled. They have not. They need to understand that things were done in order to impress and win each other. You spent money that you normally wouldn't spend. You had conversations that you normally wouldn't have. You did all of those things. Then, after a few months of marriage, you changed. Why would you think she would not change? We get comfortable after we get to know each other. It's then that we realize the real work starts when the eyelashes come off. The real work starts when the wig comes off. The real work starts when the weave is unplatted. The real work starts when you understand that this individual you are hooked up with is not all that she seemed to be in the dating and the honeymoon stage, and neither are you. That's when the real work starts.

WHAT IF THERE IS NO CEREMONY?

That's what's wrong with shacking. It furthers an illusion. People who think that they can find out what a person is like without making a commitment are only fooling themselves. Living with someone is a setup, because an individual will always change after you get married. It sets you up to live as married singles. Living together before marriage creates an atmosphere where oneness is undermined. The "you pay this bill, and I'll pay that bill" and "this is yours, and that is mine" mentality sets in. If that's in your marriage, I'm telling you, you need to begin to get counseling to work through this issue, because the Bible says, "Two shall become one."

And Jacob did so, and fulfilled her week: and he gave him Rachel his daughter to wife also.
Genesis 29:28

Jacob finally marries Rachel! A man who loves a woman will wed before any sexual encounter. Jacob is able to conclude, "Listen, Rachel. You are going to be my partner in sickness and health, poverty and wealth, 'til death do us part. I realize you are the one that God has for me for all the rest of my days. I understand that we will come together and consummate our marriage, and we'll have children, because God wants us to procreate. We'll have pleasure, because that's the second reason God gave us marriage."

Men, you must understand all of this and recognize that marriage is designed to show the world what a family ought to be. Through our unity and commitment to each other, we become a picture of Christ's relationship to His church.

Like Jacob, I have come to understand all of these things. When a man loves a woman, he marries her.

Chapter Eleven

WHEN A MAN LOVES A WOMAN
He Warns Her of Potential Threats to Their Relationship

> *And when Rachel saw that she bare Jacob no children, Rachel envied her sister; and said unto Jacob, Give me children, or else I die. And Jacob's anger was kindled against Rachel.*
>
> *Genesis 30:1–2*

Jacob's anger is righteous indignation, according to Ephesians 5:24–25. There are times when there ought to be anger—a righteous indignation. Now notice what Jacob said: "Am I in God's stead, who has withheld from thee the fruit of the womb?" I want to clarify Jacob's statement.

I Can Only Fulfill the Things I Am Responsible For!

Everything that God has given me as a responsibility in my power to do as your husband, I am going to do. When your expectations are beyond my ability to fulfill, I will let you know. Simply put, Jacob is saying, "Opening and closing the womb is God's job, not mine. Before you begin to place unrealistic expectations on me that only God can fulfill, let me get you straight."

Only Jesus

No human being can fulfill all the longings of any other person's heart:

> There is an emptiness to Eve after the Fall, and no matter how much you pour into her she will never be filled. This is where so many men falter. Either they refuse to give what they can, or they keep pouring and pouring into her and all the while feel like a failure because she is still needing more. "There are three things that are never satisfied," warns Agur son of Jakeh, "four things that never say, 'Enough!' the grave, the barren womb, land, which is never satisfied with water, and fire, which never says, 'Enough!'" The barrenness of Eve you can never hope to fill. She needs God more than she needs you, just as you need Him more than you need her! So what do you do? Offer what you have.[14]

How unfair would it be if my wife said to me, "You need to be more like Pastor Mike"? I can't be like Pastor Mike. Pastor Mike is Pastor Mike. I am Pastor Ford. I have a personality. God has given it to me. I cannot be what you want me to be if what you want is for me to be like some other man, because I'm not that other man. I'm this man. If I make thirty thousand dollars a year, don't look for a sixty-thousand-dollar lifestyle. That's far beyond what is expected. You can apply the principle in every area and every capacity. The Bible says that when a man loves a woman, he will warn her not to have unrealistic expectations. I can only be who I am.

CONCLUSION

The Chinese wanted to protect their country from invasion. They decided to build a wall so high their enemies could not climb over it, so deep they could not dig beneath it, so wide they could not dig through it, and so long they could not get around it. In all the centuries of its long history, this Great Wall of China has only been breached three times. Guess what. The enemies didn't go over, through, under, or around the Great Wall. Each time they were invaded it was because the enemy bribed a gatekeeper.

There is a wall, a standard that God has for a relationship between a man and a woman. He designed it to be impenetrable. The foundation is Jesus Christ. No one can go around it because it's so wide. The wall is too low to get under. Men are the gatekeepers. What value do you place on the safety of the city? That's the question

I am asking. What value do we as men place on our mothers, wives, daughters, girlfriends, female companions, associates, and friends?

I submit to you that if we test the climate of our society we will see that what's going on is not an action but a reaction. Women have had to react to the misuse and abuse by those who are supposed to esteem, value, and honor them! Some of the gatekeepers have been bribed! Now we must cope with the consequences of catastrophes we have created. As men we must rectify the wrong.

Timeless Principles for Successful Living

Some of you are saying that this is old-fashioned. I want you to know that godliness never goes out of style. The principles of God are always in vogue. God is saying that a man ought to be a man, and a woman ought to be a woman. Men ought to do what God designed them to do, and women likewise.

Genesis 29 affirms what God has done in creation. God is calling men to be Jacobs. Most of what Jacob did, he accomplished before Rachel became his wife. Jacob respected Rachel as a woman, and like Jacob, men need to affirm the identity, security, activity, and femininity of women in our society. Will you be a Jacob, my brother?

As men we must make a commitment to the women in our lives, before almighty God, to start today to rectify the wrongs. We must say to the Lord, "As You empower us, we will be like Jacob. We will demonstrate a Christlike love to women who are our wives, mothers, daughters, fiancées, and friends. We know that the glue that holds the family, the church, and society-at-large together is men. Lord, we come before You today broken and repentant, asking that 1 John 1:9 would be applicable in our lives. We are not saying that we are totally messed up, but we are saying that there are areas where we can improve in regard to the love we have for our women.

"And so as a testament, we commit to the fact that we are going to meet with our wives, daughters, friends, and family to try and rectify any wrongs. We want to restore emotions and relationships that have been damaged. We want to restore the material provisions that may have been taken away. We want to rectify as much as we can, knowing we can't do anything unless You empower us. So, Lord, fill us with Your Holy Spirit so that He who is resident will become president, and empower us so that we would have a change of character, conduct, and conversation. So much so that our wives, mothers, daughters, and friends will be converted. We thank You, O Lord, for the privilege to stand and make this pledge.

"Thank You in advance for granting our request.

"We pray these things in Jesus' name,

"Amen."

ENDNOTES

1. Susan Harter, "Causes and Consequences of Low Self-Esteem in Children and Adolescents," in *Self-Esteem: The Puzzle of Low Self-Regard,* ed. R.F. Baumeister (New York: Plenum, 1993), 95–96.

2. Karen Lee-Thorp and Cynthia Hicks. *Why Beauty Matters* (Colorado Springs: Navpress, 1997).

3. Edith Deen, *All the Women in the Bible* (San Francisco: Harper, 1988).

4. Karen Lee-Thorp and Cynthia Hicks. *Why Beauty Matters.*

5. Gary Smalley and John Trent, *The Gift of the Blessing* (Nashville: Thomas Nelson, 1993).

6. Harvey Richard Schiffman, *Sensation and Perception: An Integrated Approach* (New York: John Wiley & Sons, 1982), 107.

7. Dolores Krieger, "Therapeutic Touch: The Imprimatur of Nursing" *American Journal of Nursing* (May, 1975), 784.

8. UCLA Monthly, Alumni Association News (March-April 1981), 1.

9. Dr. Myles Munroe, *Understanding the Purpose and Power of a Man* (Kensington, Pa.: Whitaker House, 2002), 221.

10. Ibid.

11. John Eldredge, *Wild at Heart* (Nashville: Thomas Nelson, 2001).

12. Hazel Felleman, ed., *The Best Loved Poems of the American People* (New York: Doubleday. 1936).

13. Willard F. Harley, Jr., *His Needs Her Needs* (Grand Rapids: Fleming H. Revell, 1988), 32.

14. John Eldredge, *Wild at Heart.*

BIBLIOGRAPHY

Bilezikian, Gilbert. *Beyond Sex Roles: What the Bible Says about a Woman's Place in Church and Family.* Grand Rapids: Baker, 1985.

Brand, Dr. Paul, and Philip Yancey. *The Gift of Pain: Why We Hurt and What We Can do About it.* Grand Rapids: Zondervan, 1997.

Eldredge, John. *Wild at Heart. Discovering the Secrets of a Man's Soul.* Nashville: Nelson, 2001.

Felleman, Hazel, ed., *Best Loved Poems of the American People. Selected poem* by Ray Croft. New York: Doubleday, 1936.

Harley, Willard F., Jr. *His Needs, Her Needs: Building an Affair-Proof Marriage.* Grand Rapids: Revell, 1988.

Harter, Susan. "Causes and Consequences of Low Self-Esteem in Children and Adolescents," in *Self-Esteem: The Puzzle of Low Self-Regard,* ed. R.F. Baumeister. New York: Plenum, 1993.

Krupp, Joanne. *Woman: God's Plan Not Man's Tradition.* Salem, OR: Preparing the Way Publishers, 1999.

Lee-Thorp, Karen, and Cynthia Hicks. *Why Beauty Matters.* Colorado Springs: NavPress, 1997.

Munroe, Dr. Myles. *Understanding the Purpose and Power of Men: A Book for Men and the Women Who Love Them.* New Kensington, PA: Whitaker House, 2001.

Pride, Mary. *The Way Home: Beyond Feminism, Back to Reality.* Westchester, IL: Crossway, 1985.

Rainey, Dennis. *Lonely Husbands, Lonely Wives: Rekindling Intimacy in Every Marriage.* Dallas:Word, 1989.

Reece, Colleen L. Women of the Bible. *Fifty Biographical sketches of Biblical Women.* Uhrichsville, OH: Barbour and Company.

Schiffman, Harvey Richard. *Sensation and Perception: An Integrated Approach.* New York: John Wiley & Sons, 1982.

Seamands, David A. *Living with Your Dreams: Let God Restore Your Shattered Dreams.* Wheaton, IL: Victor Books, 1990.

Smalley, Gary and Trent, Dr. John. *The Gift of the Blessing.* Nashville: Thomas Nelson, 1993.

Yorkey, Mike, ed. *Growing a Healthy Home.* Brentwood, TN: Wolgemuth & Hyatt, 1990.

The Negro National Anthem

Lift every voice and sing
Till earth and heaven ring,
Ring with the harmonies of Liberty;
Let our rejoicing rise
High as the listening skies,
Let it resound loud as the rolling sea.
Sing a song full of the faith that the dark past has taught us,
Sing a song full of the hope that the present has brought us,
Facing the rising sun of our new day begun
Let us march on till victory is won.

So begins the Black National Anthem, by James Weldon Johnson in 1900. Lift Every Voice is the name of the joint imprint of The Institute for Black Family Development and Moody Publishers.
Our vision is to advance the cause of Christ through publishing African-American Christians who educate, edify, and disciple Christians in the church community through quality books written for African Americans.

The Institute for Black Family Development is a national Christian organization. It offers degreed and nondegreed training nationally and internationally to established and emerging leaders from churches and Christian organizations. To learn more about The Institute for Black Family Development write us at:

15151 Faust
Detroit, Michigan 48223

Since 1894, *Moody Publishers* has been dedicated to equip and motivate people to advance the cause of Christ by publishing evangelical Christian literature and other media for all ages, around the world. Because we are a ministry of the Moody Bible Institute of Chicago, a portion of the proceeds from the sale of this book go to train the next generation of Christian leaders. If we may serve you in any way in your spiritual journey toward understanding Christ and the Christian life, please contact us at:

820 N. LaSalle Blvd.
Chicago, Illinois 60610
www.moodypublishers.com

WHEN A MAN LOVES A WOMAN TEAM

ACQUIRING EDITOR
Cynthia Ballenger

COPY EDITOR
Amanda Johnson

BACK COVER COPY
Anne Perdicaris

COVER DESIGN
SolidRoxMedia

COVER PHOTO
PhotoDisc/Fotosearch

INTERIOR DESIGN
Ragont Design

PRINTING AND BINDING
Versa Press, Inc.

The typeface for the text of this book is
Sabon